More Praise for
108 Metaphors for Mindfulness

"Live in accord with the advice inside
and your life will change."
—Rev. Taihaku Gretchen Priest,
founder of Shao Shan Spiritual Temple

"This book belongs in the curriculum of every clinical
training program and should be recommended to anyone
who wants to learn to live in the mindful moment."
—William J. McCann, PsyD,
director of Behavioral Science Education,
Wake Forest Baptist Medical Center

"If you contemplate these brief stories, your emotional
intelligence and mindfulness will develop effortlessly
from the insights they provide."
—Polly Young-Eisendrath, PhD,
author of *The Resilient Spirit*

"A wonderful collection and a wild ride!"
—Thomas Bien, PhD, author of *Mindful Therapy*

108 Metaphors for Mindfulness

108 METAPHORS
FOR MINDFULNESS

from Wild Chickens to Petty Tyrants

Arnie Kozak, PhD

Wisdom Publications
199 Elm Street
Somerville MA 02144 USA
wisdompubs.org

Library of Congress Cataloging-in-Publication Data
Names: Kozak, Arnold, author.
   Title: 108 metaphors for mindfulness : from wild chickens to petty tyrants /
      Arnold Kozak, PhD.
   Other titles: Wild chickens and petty tyrants | One hundred and eight
      metaphors for mindfulness
   Description: 2 [edition]. | Somerville : Wisdom Publications, 2016. | Rev.
      ed. of: Wild chickens and petty tyrants : 108 metaphors for mindfulness.
      c2009. | Includes bibliographical references.
   Identifiers: LCCN 2016004204| ISBN 9781614293835 (pbk. : alk. paper) | ISBN
      161429383X (pbk. : alk. paper)
   Subjects: LCSH: Mindfulness-based cognitive therapy. | Metaphor—Religious
      aspects—Buddhism. | Meditation—Buddhism.
   Classification: LCC RC489.M55 K69 2016 | DDC 616.89/1425—dc23
   LC record available at http://lccn.loc.gov/2016004204

ISBN 978-1-61429-383-5   ebook ISBN 978-1-61429-399-6

20 19 18 17 16
5 4 3 2 1

Cover design by Philip Pascuzzo. Set in Sabon 11/15.

Please visit fscus.org.

In memory of McCoy and Sondra

Table of Contents

Metaphors for Self

Metaphors for Emotion, Change, and "Ordinary Craziness"

Metaphors for Acceptance, Resistance, and Space

Metaphors for Practice

Preface

Since the initial publication of *108 Metaphors for Mindfulness* in 2009, I've come to appreciate further the Buddha's mastery with metaphors. Indeed, Buddhist scholar Damien Keown said, "The Buddha's skill in teaching the Dharma, demonstrated in his ability to adapt his message to the context in which it was delivered. Parables, metaphors, and similes formed an important part of his teaching repertoire, skillfully tailored to suit the level of his audience." The Pali Canon, which is the written record of the Buddha's teachings, contains over 1000 metaphorical references addressing over 500 different concepts. He used metaphors of elements (especially water and fire), animals, and the technologies of his time (for example, arrows) to match his teachings to his audience.

The aim of this book is to follow in the footsteps Buddha's metaphorical pedagogy in my own small way. The power of metaphor is a breathing presence for me, and I offer these 108 metaphors to help mindfulness come alive for you. I hope this metaphorical approach—which I continue in *Mindfulness A to Z: 108 Insights for Awakening Now*—helps to bring mindfulness even further into the mainstream.

Mindful America: The Mutual Transformation of Buddhist Meditation and American Culture, by Jeff Wilson, is the first historical critique of the mindfulness movement. *Wild Chickens and Petty Tyrants* was featured in his chapter on "Mainstreaming Mindfulness." Professor Wilson said, "[Kozak's] metaphors typically draw on elements of everyday life or mainstream American culture, often with the benefits that can be drawn from mindfulness practice." While some Buddhist scholars see the popularizing of mindfulness as problematic, I was pleased to see my book featured in this way because it is precisely my intention to bring mindfulness to a wider audience.

As in the Buddha's time, metaphors help to make the teachings accessible to anyone and everyone—and I hope they do this for you.

Introduction

In 1988, my doctoral advisor in clinical psychology introduced me to a slim volume *Metaphors We Live By*, by the linguist George Lakoff and the philosopher Mark Johnson. This incisive work shaped the course of my graduate education and changed the way I think about and practice psychotherapy.

Metaphors help us to understand the world: they are the workhorse of language and meaning, letting us understand one thing in terms of another and helping us to communicate our understanding to others. We understand the world by metaphor and by doing so create a sense of the familiar. Yet metaphors are far more than colorful devices of language. In fact, they cannot be separated from the way we see and even experience the world. What's more, much of our everyday language is based metaphorically on our physical bodies—our embodiment—and many metaphors reflect, after a fashion, the way the human brain is organized. In this way, concepts are not arbitrary references but reflect how we are built, the very structure of our being.

The psychologist Julian Jaynes argued that metaphor is the very ground of language. Take for example the verb *to be*. This basic verb is used in sentences such as "I am" and "she is." It is derived from the Sanskrit *bhu*, which means "to grow" or "to make grow." Thus, *to be* has the same etymological root as another Sanskrit verb *asmi*, which means "to breathe." And here, encapsulated in the language of an ancient metaphor, we see that living and breathing are one. And, in poignant connection to themes in the rest of this book, we can also reflect on the fact that the process of breathing is the foundation of mindfulness meditation, and by extension mindfulness is itself a practice of *being*.

This book presents 108 metaphors for mindfulness, meditation practice, self, change, deep acceptance, and other related concepts. I have compiled the metaphors presented here over decades of meditating, practicing yoga, studying Buddhism, and being a mental health professional.

Mindfulness is a process of self-inquiry directed at what is happening in the moment, often focused on how the body feels, on how we *embody* this moment. Mindfulness is an intentional directing of attention to experience as it unfolds in the present moment, one moment following the next—the very happening of experience as it is happening without inner commentary, judgment, or storytelling.

And metaphors are indispensable to understand mindfulness, and to help make it a part of everyday life. Metaphors for mindfulness can motivate us to practice, show us how to bring mindfulness into daily life, and help us to employ mindfulness to transform our life.

I often find myself thinking and speaking in metaphor, and many of these metaphors were created in the midst of my clinical work. Imagery in metaphors anchors understanding, and is often a guide to the change necessary for self-improvement. These metaphors give the people I treat and teach a bridge from the conceptual to the experiential.

Many of the metaphors in this book are original to me; others are selected from the literature on mindfulness and Buddhism. The metaphors on the following pages form the practical core of my mindfulness teaching. Each metaphor is a node in a network of interweaving concepts that attempt to enliven the experience of mindfulness. And what's more, you'll also find that even the process of "unfolding" and elaborating one metaphor requires the use of several more!

Reading This Book

Each of the 108 entries can stand alone, so feel free to skip around. They are organized into five sections: Metaphors for Mind; Metaphors for Self; Metaphors for Emotion, Change, and "Ordinary Craziness"; Metaphors for Acceptance, Resistance, and Space; and Metaphors for Practice. As with any categorization system, there is much overlap between the metaphors—especially, it's interesting to note, those for self and mind. Nevertheless, these categories provide a general organization that might be helpful to the reader.

We can think of these metaphors as seeds. Reading them will plant them in the soil of your experience with the aspiration that they will take root and bear fruit in your life.

Metaphors for Mind

How can the mind be described? How can the mind be known? Try to describe the mind without referring to something else. It's hard to do this. The mind can certainly move around; for example: "my mind was racing" or "my mind just wandered." The mind can talk and tell stories; for example: "Oh my god, what have I done?" or "He always does this, when will he learn?" The mind can vex us in so many ways: convincing us that we are defective in some way or making the case that someone else is insufferable and must change. The mind's tendency to be automatic—in the way it talks to itself in habitual ways, and the ways it chases thoughts, feelings, and perceptions without reflection—is also a recurrent theme.

When it comes to the experience of mindfulness and mindfulness meditation, there is almost no other way to describe them other than by using metaphor. George Lakoff and Mark Johnson in their theoretical tome *Philosophy in the Flesh* put it this way:

> It is virtually impossible to think or talk about the mind in any serious way without conceptualizing it metaphorically. Whenever we conceptualize aspects of mind in terms of grasping ideas, reaching conclusions, being unclear, or swallowing a claim, we are using metaphor to make sense of what we do with our minds.

One essential message here is that what you take to be the mind cannot be separated from what you take to be the body. The mind-body duality instigated by the philosopher Descartes more than three hundred years ago has been a lasting but difficult legacy. Indeed, both mind and self are concepts critical to mindfulness that are impossible to describe and understand without the metaphors that come out of our embodied experience. And mindfulness meditation can bring you closer to your embodiment because during meditation, you notice how your body feels in the moment. Mindfulness can help you to become intimate with the vast wisdom of feelings. Mindfulness can, therefore, bring you closer to reality and can help you to overcome the false duality of mind and body.

Metaphors for mind and mindfulness can help to bring you closer to the ground of experience—the physical body that is also mind. From this perspective, mindfulness practice is a form of rational behavior that helps to reveal the embodied basis of mental life.

Even the term *mindfulness* is itself metaphorical. What does it mean to be "full of mind"—or empty of it? In fact the term *mindfulness* itself stems from a metaphor that sees the mind as a container: things can be put "into" the mind; advice can go "in one ear and out the other"; and you can "draw a blank" in trying to remember someone's name.

This section on Metaphors for Mind explores many different ways you might understand the elusive mind in terms of other things.

1. Storytelling Mind

Do you tend to think in words, often lengthy and unnecessary, and talk to yourself and others in the privacy of your mind? Of course, you do; we all do. These conversations often form larger stories, patterns, and models of the world. It is as if there is an ongoing narrative to consciousness. The automatic thinking mind can get you into all sorts of trouble. This is what I call the *storytelling mind*.

It is useful to make a distinction between the deliberate intentional mind and the storytelling mind. The deliberate intentional mind is practical and reality-based. Storytelling mind is impractical and often distorted or circular, often repeating itself *ad nauseum*. One of the favorite pastimes of the storytelling mind is "jumping" to conclusions.

Here is an example of the storytelling mind in action that occurred during a meditation retreat that I led in the middle of an eight-week training sequence for a small group of physicians. The retreat was scheduled for both Saturday and Sunday. As far as I could tell, Saturday had gone well, with silent sitting and walking meditation throughout the day and a discussion period at the end. I arrived at my office early Sunday morning in anticipation of the group's arrival. A little while after the appointed starting time, no one had showed up. I was beginning to grow concerned and my storytelling mind took wing. "Oh no, they really must have *hated* yesterday because they didn't even call to say there weren't coming." "I must have pushed everyone too hard and they've had enough of meditating…" And so my thoughts went, on and on and on. Then reality burst in and my helpful mind spoke up and reminded me that *I had yet to unlock the front door!* I rushed out to find everyone happily conversing on the sidewalk in front of my office.

Mindfulness practice will get you on intimate terms with your storytelling mind (or what neuroscientists term the default-mode network). Your storytelling mind will take you out of the present 99 times out of 100, and you'll frequently notice your storytelling mind during meditation. You'll be watching and feeling your breathing, and then all of sudden you'll realize that you've been lost in thinking. When you recognize this, you come back to the breath. Dealing with the storytelling mind during meditation practice helps you to deal with everyday stresses and strains. By paying attention to how the mind goes into this particular form of distraction, you train yourself to notice it and then you'll have an opportunity to come back.

As a result, you'll be more engaged in the present and less lost in a mind full of stories.

2. The Four-Story Building

To explain the mind in a simplified and straightforward manner to my patients, I devised a four-level explanation. I use this model to explain how mindfulness can be helpful in changing the "center of gravity" of where you spend most of your time—from the "fourth floor" to the "ground floor."

The first floor, the floor resting firmly on the "ground" of being, is what is occurring now. This is the level of sensation, of your sensory organs and the brain receiving information from the world, including from within the body. The second floor is perception, the information the mind "distills" from sensation. At this level, the brain identifies what has been sensed and begins to put it into categories. This is highly adaptive, and certainly not unique to human brains; even amoebae are capable of rudimentary categorization. Categorization is a convenient, efficient, and adaptive way of dealing with what would otherwise be overwhelming amounts of information.

When describing this level in a classroom setting, I point out that when the people present entered the classroom for the first time they instantly recognized, for example, that the chairs are indeed chairs—and, accordingly, sat in them. Instead of seeing blobs of colors and shapes (what is happening on the first floor), they saw objects that fit the categories in their minds for *chairs*.

Not a microsecond after this efficient and adaptive categorization, the "feeling-tone" and "value" of the perception is registered as pleasant, unpleasant, or neutral. This is the "third floor"—evaluation. The third floor tells us what is useful to approach and what may be life-preserving to avoid and is also, of course, highly adaptive.

And finally, we arrive at the "fourth floor"—the thinking and talking part of the mind. This fourth floor has two "departments"—which we might name the deliberate and the non-deliberate, automatic part. The deliberate department is the crowning glory of human capacity. It includes the ability to solve problems, synthesize, plan, and create. The automatic department of the thinking and talking mind on the fourth floor tends to be repetitive, narrowly focused, and anxiety-ridden.

In this metaphor, it is most stable and "grounding" for us to "live" as close to the first floor of our four-story building as we can. This ground floor is closest to reality and closest to our lived experience. Mindfulness is the elevator or staircase that allows you to "return" to the grounded floor of experience from the fourth story of, if you'll pardon the pun, "stories." Yet none of this is to suggest we raze the other stories. These all have their functions.

Consider this basic method for using mindfulness to navigate the floors. Start by looking at an unpleasant reaction to an event that you have had. On the first floor, there is the event: perhaps the event is falling on the ice. Then the brain has to recognize what has happened (perception, categorization). On the second floor is pain as a pure experience. The brain is well equipped to recognize pain and to do so is functional. There is key information in this experience, and the "ouch" that comes on the third floor brings this message home. The first three floors are traversed in a microsecond. Then, most of the time is spent in the loft of the fourth floor.

Beyond any practical measures such as brushing yourself off, checking for cuts, and so forth, there is not much to do. Yet the mind is just getting started. There may be thoughts that start with the invective "Oh my god..." or "I can't believe I just did that; what a stupid idiot." There may be an entire dramatic narrative created in response to the original event that has you paralyzed and homeless before you know it (this is known as catastrophic thinking). Ask yourself, "Is this thinking valuable? Is it necessary?" If the answer to these questions is no, it might be time to start walking the stairs back down.

To get downstairs, ask "How does my body actually feel, right now?" By this I mean, how does the actual body feel beyond your *idea* of the body? Making this distinction—noticing the difference between physical sensations and thoughts about the body—may take some practice. Much of mindfulness practice involves wresting the mind out of thoughts and bringing it into the felt experience of the here and now as the physical sensations in the body. And this is how we start to experience the fruits of mindfulness.

Almost one hundred years ago, William James noted, "The intellectual life of man consists almost wholly in his substitution of a conceptual order for the perceptual order in which his experience originally lives." Mindfulness offers the possibility of living closer to this perceptual order.

3. Commentarial Mind

A cartoon in *The New Yorker* features two couples at a movie theater. The man sitting in front turns to the couple behind him who are talking through the movie and says, "If we wanted running commentary, we'd have waited for the DVD."

As you probably know (and at the always grave risk of over-explaining a joke), DVDs of recent movies often come with a "director's commentary," where the director, one of the actors, or others involved in the making of the film comment upon the action of the film. The movie plays in the background at a muted volume as the director's voice-over provides a personal take on the whats, whys, and wherefores of the film.

In similar fashion, the mind provides the same sort of running, scene-by-scene commentary. As a result, our life itself becomes merely background, at muted volume, and the mind chatters on—making comments, passing judgment, and rendering opinions.

Mindfulness offers you an alternative to the director's commentary and to a life muted by ceaseless commentary—an alternative to the commentarial mind. Your life exists in full, vivid color and symphonic volume in every moment, and you can make contact with it whenever the running commentary ceases. This kind of commentary is almost always present, and rarely questioned. Yet so often it is engaged as an essentially pointless, valueless endeavor, reviewing the same details and scenarios over and over again. And other times the tenor and flavor of the commentarial mind runs to danger with thoughts of anxiety, or visions of a future warped by dire predictions of catastrophe and demise. In these cases, the commentarial mind can wreak havoc on our lives, detracting and distracting us from the rich, vivid present. On these occasions, it is imperative to place a moratorium on commentary—lest we compound our misery. Mindfulness is the tool we use to do this. It lets us take a break from the scene-by-scene of judging good and bad, telling ourselves what we like and dislike, and beating ourselves up for every imperfection and imagined slight.

4. Doggy Mind and Monkey Mind

Doggy Mind runs after bone.
Monkey Mind swings from tree to tree.

This little verse encapsulates two of our most common conditioned tendencies of mind.

Have you ever noticed how some dogs, such as Labrador Retrievers, will run ceaselessly after a bone—even a plastic one? Larry Rosenberg, a meditation teacher and author of the classic *Breath by Breath*, observed a friend's dog behaving in this manner and likened it to a state of the mind with which we are all intimately familiar. Often we may be like the dog running after every bone—every impulse, desire, aversion—that comes across our mind. Any thought can occasion the chase. This is doggy mind.

The monkey is another animal metaphor for the mind. The monkey mind swings from tree to tree, from thought to thought to thought. Monkey mind is active, restless, and wild. Whether it is the doggy mind or the monkey mind, this restless activity is encountered when you first start to do mindfulness meditation practice, and frequently after as well.

But it's important to recognize that the goal in meditation is not to eradicate thinking—we do not need to cage doggy mind and monkey mind. The goal is to *observe* what is going on in the mind. By watching thinking as a process (that is, noticing it is happening) instead of engaging in the content of thinking (that is, what thinking is saying and meaning), you might notice a tendency for the incessant movement of thinking to diminish. After all, doggy and monkey mind thrive on attention.

Like stray animals, if you feed them, they will always return, wanting more. If you are constantly feeding your thoughts by paying attention to their content, they too will keep coming back. See what happens if you simply watch the dog chasing a bone or the monkey swinging from branch to branch—and don't follow along.

5. Lion Mind

Lion Mind is unimpressed.

The image of the lion gives us insight into two other ways the mind might function.

The lion mind is concentrated and focused. It is calm and dispassionate, king of the jungle, lord of its domain. It ignores the bones that were so compelling to the doggy mind. Being a big cat, it demurs and stays solidly put. Having lion mind can be a helpful outcome of mindfulness meditation practice—but I do not encourage seeking this as a goal, but instead allowing it to emerge naturally and over time from practicing mindfulness. The goal of practice is not to sit still, impervious like the lion, but to *practice coming back* to the present over and over again. Paradoxically, when you are least lion-like you have the most opportunities to come back to the present. This returning to the present, again and again, is the key value of mindfulness training.

Whereas if lion mind—in the form of peace and disengagement—is aimed for too early and aggressively in practice, it can be detrimental to future learning. The instructions for mindfulness are very precise, if deceptively straightforward. Pay attention to what is happening now and, when attention has wandered from now, bring it back (and do so without rancor, regret, or recrimination). Notice there is nothing about peacefulness, nothing even about relaxation, in these instructions. Relaxation can be a reliable by-product of practice, but it is *not* the goal of practice. Becoming intimate with your mind is the goal of practice. If your mind is in fury, is agitated, is lost—that is the mind that you work with. Again, I see this as the real payoff to practice because it most resembles the mind off the cushion in day-to-day situations.

The lion mind may require conditions to support it such as a quiet place to practice, a break from urgent responsibilities, and so forth. This type of environment can be provided at a meditation retreat—a protected place to practice can be valuable. However, the drawback and limitation to this is that you, like most people, probably cannot live in a retreat environment. You probably live in a busy, chaotic world, filled with children and parents, deadlines, and responsibilities. This is the environment where you want mindfulness practice to pay dividends. Therefore, in something of a paradox, it is your familiarity and ease with the doggy mind that will help you to integrate mindfulness into the fabric of everyday life.

It is precisely by knowing doggy mind that lion mind is cultivated. This is not to diminish the value of the lion mind. The lion mind will come with continued practice and it establishes the foundation for later insights.

6. Friendly Neighborhood Spider Mind

Spider Mind weaves endless webs.

Training the mind brings it from the chaotic and opportunistic doggy mind to the regal, quiet, and stable lion mind, to the active and engaged yet unattached spider mind. There is a Zen saying—"In the beginning, the mountains are mountains, and the rivers are rivers." And then, it is said, with practice, "the mountains are no longer mountains and the rivers are no longer rivers." This comes as meditation shifts the mind's relationship to the perceived world. However, this is not the end of the story. With continued practice, "the mountains are once again mountains and the rivers are once again rivers." This is the enlightenment of the ordinary mind.

Popular images of "enlightenment" can get in the way of learning mindfulness. Enlightenment is often portrayed as an epic or cosmic psychological event, with fireworks going off, bells ringing, and a state of permanent mystical transcendence. Once enlightened, the individual's being is irrevocably transformed. But in a way, enlightenment is the ego's biggest disappointment. No bells, no fireworks, just this moment, and then the next. Just mountains, and just rivers.

Moreover, as with the lion mind, if your *goal* is enlightenment, you have set up a condition that prevents the goal. One cannot usefully *strive* for enlightenment. Yet, it will flow directly out of practice.

Spider mind embodies the quality of engaged attention that at the same time is not caught up in the tales of storytelling mind, in endless judgments of commentarial mind, or in the restless jumping and chasing of doggy and monkey mind. The spider mind has a different relationship to distress than the doggy mind. The spider mind is passionate, dispassionate, and compassionate all at the same time.

An erroneous stereotype of Buddhist enlightenment is that it makes you desire-less or passion-less. This stereotype is an unfortunate consequence of the language that is used to describe attachment, desire, and emptiness. However, the spider mind does not become apathetic and lose interest in the material world. On the contrary, the Spider mind has all of its energy and resources available for engagement and can do so freely and with vigor. What is unique to the Spider mind is not the actions it takes but the *quality of mind* that accompanies those actions.

People taking my eight-week mindfulness-based stress reduction/cognitive therapy course sometimes worry they will lose their personality by meditating. I joke that they are not Z.I.T.—Zombies-In-Training! I try to disabuse people of this notion that somehow not being attached to outcomes will make them apathetic, flat, or utterly without a sense of humor. Quite the opposite, by freeing the mind from its usual mental burdens you are free to engage with vigor, and realize who you actually are beyond all the anxious and limiting things you tell yourself—and life becomes joyful and endlessly amusing.

While the spider mind is fully engaged, it is not fixated on outcome. It does not whine and moan when things don't go its way. It does not feel deprived or disappointed, trying to hold on to whatever it has in vain. The spider mind lives in the present moment. And most important of all: spider mind doesn't take itself too seriously.

7. Carving Nature at the Joints

A good classification system is said to "carve nature at the joints." That is, it groups things more or less the way they exist in nature, dividing them in naturally sensible ways. The joints are easier to cut, as I learned one summer in high school where my job was cutting up whole chickens into pieces for frying.

A cartoon in *The New Yorker* portrays a group of dogs with nametags hanging from their rear ends. The categories we humans use are, of course, relative to human perceptual apparatus (that is, we use names and don't sniff each other's behinds). Further-more, categories are critical to functioning. Yet, is it possible that you will lose the flavor of life when you impose your categories in super-efficient ways? Ronald Reagan is purported to have said, "If you've seen one redwood tree, you've seen them all." That's an efficient attitude for a Paleolithic hunter-gatherer but is this how you want to live now? How you pay attention is important because it is not just redwood trees that could be clumped together but major portions of your life—moments, days, and long stretches of life such as "middle-age."

There is a cost to automatic categorization. While such learning is efficient, it restricts information and changes the experience of time. Indeed, as neuroscientist Daniel J. Siegel explains:

> In many ways such learning oppresses our raw sensory experience by muddying the waters of clear perceptions with prior expectation. As we grow into adulthood, it is very likely that these accumulated layers of perceptual models and conceptual categories constrict subjective time and deaden our feelings of being alive. Without the intentional effort to awaken, life speeds by. We habituate to experience perceiving through the filter of the past

and not orienting ourselves to novel distinctions of the present.

Mindfulness practice will help you to examine your learned automatic categories and to revise or dismantle them if they don't fit or work any longer. You can choose. Mindfulness will help you to find a richness that exists in the difference of things and in how things change dynamically. Backing away from automatic categorization accomplishes this. You can experience things as they are when the category moves into the background.

8. "You've Got Mail!"

I'm willing to venture that you don't look through every spam email or scour over every piece of junk snail mail you receive. If you did, you'd likely never get anything else done, as you'd be spending your entire day being fascinated by offers for Cialis, unclaimed sweepstakes, and the latest stock tip to make you rich. Instead of reading through each email with fascination, you quickly recognize it as spam or junk and delete or ignore it. Better yet, you have a program that does it for you.

Mindfulness is to the mind what a spam blocker is to your inbox. By practicing mindfulness, you become familiar and intimate with the functioning of your mind. By doing so, you can quickly recognize "junk thoughts" when they occur, disentangle yourself from them, and minimize the clutter. By getting into the habit of not becoming engrossed in every thought that the mind encounters, the burdensome thoughts themselves may become less frequent visitors, as if you were "unsubscribing" from various junk mail distribution lists.

9. The Inner Mute Button

Many people use their remote controls to mute commercials on TV. I have a friend who watches sports programs by muting them and listening to classical music in the background, allowing a different choreography to a football or basketball game to emerge.

What might it mean to find our own "inner mute button"—a mute button for the mind? If the mind is like a television, you can watch the television without the sound by seeing the images that pass by on the screen without getting involved in their storyline and content. You can distance yourself from the drama by allowing things to be as they are, silently and without color commentary.

The mind produces three basic types of subjective content: images or pictures, self-talk, and feelings that are bodily sensations with an emotional flavor. These can arise individually or in the various combinations of image-talk, image-feel, talk-feel, and image-talk-feel. There are also remembered or imagined sounds, such as music, which I consider another form of image space. The objective spaces for attention include sight, sound, and bodily sensations and less frequently smell and taste.

When a traumatic or difficult experience has occurred and the event is relived in all its pain and horror, there is intensity (as mediated by the closeness to the images of the experience), content (the storyline of the event), reactivity in thoughts ("Oh my god, why is this still happening to me?"), and reactivity in emotions and physiology (the embodied sensations that accompany the memories, such as rapid heartbeat, sweating, and emotional feelings). If you can watch the event as a quiet image on the mind's screen, you can create healing distance from the event.

Try this strategy whenever something distressing arises: Whatever happens, such as panic, fear, or anxiety, there will be physical feelings or sensations in the body. Try to move these physical sensations that accompany emotions and difficult situations. This attention will interrupt the unhelpful color commentary in the mental TV and it will help you to become more familiar and intimate with your body. This intervention shifts attention from the subjective mind spaces to the objective spaces, and by doing so reduces suffering.

Repeat as necessary!

10. Fierce Attention

I first heard the term Fierce Attention discussed by the poet and corporate consultant David Whyte in his *Clear Mind, Wild Heart*. It suggests that mindfulness does not need to be tranquil and passive. It can be active, precise, and strong—even fierce. This runs counter to images of serene pools and drops of water. Mindfulness can bring the unencumbered Fierce Attention of the peaceful warrior—this warrior is an ethical warrior who does no harm.

Mindfulness practice develops this fierce warrior-like attention (as well as the ethical stance that seeks to cause ever less harm). Through practicing mindfulness you can develop an accurate and courageous way of looking at everything—including your own mind. Instead of moving into and relying so heavily upon defense mechanisms such as denial, you can face what is present with calm strength and resolve.

Fierce Attention also helps you to be more efficient and creative by cutting out much of the distraction that typically plagues the mind. Fierce Attention can be useful in any context but especially when peak performance is required, for example, during athletic competition, at a presentation for work, or handling a personal or community crisis.

For me, Fierce Attention is also important when I trail run with my dog. When my attention lapses, when I begin to have imaginary conversations in my mind, I start to trip over the rocks and roots that cover the trail. One morning, after it had been raining, and the planks that cover the mud patches on the trail were slick, I got caught up in an internal conversation. The result was predictable.

These trails are treacherous and without Fierce Attention I am at peril.

11. Different Kinds of Snow

You don't have to live near the Arctic Circle to know there are different kinds of snow. In Vermont, we get everything from heavy wet snow to what snowboarders like to call "champagne powder." Like the snow, our thoughts come in a number of varieties. Some are heavy and sticky like wet snow and some are like the dry, fluffy crystals of champagne powder.

Mood and energy level can influence how sticky the "snow of the mind" is. Being a little stressed, depressed, anxious, or tired tends to make for thoughts that might feel somehow heavy and sodden. Thoughts glom on to one another and make terrific snowballs that are efficient projectiles. If you throw these snowballs at others or get hit by one yourself, it could be dangerous. Be careful!

Mindfulness practice tends to make the snow into champagne powder—light, fluffy, and dry—great for enjoyable skiing. Yet if you've ever tried to pack this kind of snow into a snowball, you'll know that the flakes rarely stick to each other in dangerous or unwieldy masses. With snow like that it is hard to hurt anyone, including yourself.

Mindfulness practice helps to prevent "thought-flakes" from sticking together—and keeps the slopes of your mind safe and easily maneuvered on.

12. Waking Up

The story of the Buddha's awakening provides the metaphor of seeing into the nature of the way things actually are as a kind of "waking up" from a dream of suffering.

After his long period of searching and ascetic practice in which he nearly starved to death, Siddhartha Gautama accepted some sweet rice on a banana leaf from a young girl and, with the strength of this nourishment, endeavored to sit under the Bodhi Tree until he attained enlightenment. Some time later, he achieved his goal.

From this enlightenment experience, he articulated the Four Noble Truths. Briefly, the Four Noble Truths set out how suffering or dissatisfaction is to a large degree self-inflicted when we don't recognize the changing nature of things. This is an optimistic insight. While the way we tend to relate to the world creates this unhappiness, we have it within ourselves to do something about it. Mindfulness is an integral component of the path out of suffering. According to legend, the results of his meditation and insights made him *radiant*—a word that expresses another metaphor for en*light*enment. When people saw him, they would stop him and ask, "Who are you? Are you a god or a man?" Siddhartha answered, "I am *buddho*," which translates into "I am awake." Thus, he was called the Buddha, the Awakened One.

If there is a need to awaken, were you asleep before? Are you asleep now? When you live inside the storytelling mind, you are separated from the world of experiences. When you are on automatic pilot, you are the opposite of wakefulness. Some have called this state of sleep "consensus trance." Have you ever noticed how you can go through your day without making eye contact with people? I have noticed this, especially with relatively anonymous encounters with store clerks. I always pause with my head raised and eyes ready to engage them after the transaction. However, they are often not there to meet my eyes. Where are they? Asleep? Protecting themselves? And if so, from what?

What can we wake up to? Can we wake up to life in this moment—even if it is painful or difficult? Can we even wake up to life in this moment when it is pleasant and wonderful? To wake up is to "show up" for your life. As Jon Kabat-Zinn reminds us, in the contest of life, "You must be present to win." Mindfulness practice offers a method and set of skills to wake you up.

When you pay attention to your experience in the moment, you are awake. When you are feeling the whole of your embodied mental experience (or bodymind) instead of just identifying with one part—usually the thinking part—you are awake.

The more you practice the more you will notice how asleep you have been. When mindfulness starts to become a habit you will start to notice how the mind actually functions. You may be astounded how often you are lost in thoughts and asleep. Seeing that you are lost is the first step toward waking up. Keep at it!

13. "Next Stop: 110th Street"

Imagine you are standing on a subway platform in New York City. A train pulls up to a screeching stop. You step on the train without looking. You don't know where the train is going or if it will take you to your destination. You just get on without any awareness.

How often do you get on the subway car of thoughts and stories and get taken away to places where you did not intend or want to be? Thoughts have this compelling quality and sometimes have a pressured quality like the driving force of a train. Unfortunately, some thought patterns, especially those associated with anxiety and depression, can take you to these unwanted places where discomfort and dissatisfaction prevail, and indeed grow stronger. You can spend large portions of your day, and even your life, riding on "trains of thought" that don't bring you to where you'd like to go.

When you practice mindfulness meditation, you'll get out of the habit of getting on unwanted trains—or at least noticing when you've boarded and then getting off at the next possible stop. During meditation practice, you may see the thoughts pulling into the station. From the vantage point of meditation, which is both the posture and your intention for practice, you can then watch the train pull out again without jumping on. Thoughts, like subway cars, come and go regularly. There will always be another train later if you miss this one.

And perhaps sometimes you'll choose to emerge from the buried subway and just walk to your destination in the sun!

14. "Man Goes Over Niagara Falls in a Barrel"

The mind is like a waterfall. Think of a waterfall's properties. There is a great flow of water from a river and a freefall over a rocky ledge. The water moves with great force and always reaches the bottom. The mind can have this sort of flow with many thoughts moving with great force. Where are you in relationship to this flow? Are you in a barrel headed over the falls? Or, are you standing—as you might at the bottom of Niagara Falls—safely in a cave behind the falls watching the spectacle?

The process of watching the fall of thoughts from a safe place is called "decentering" or "disidentification." Distance from the ferocity and power of the thoughts creates a kind of insulating safety. The thoughts may continue to rage like the water of Niagara Falls, but your relationship to these thoughts can change when you "decenter" from them. You do this by not getting into that barrel and hurtling away. In this way, it is possible for distressing thoughts to become less distressing.

Mindfulness practice helps to establish a safe vantage point from which to observe the copious flow of the mind. At first, you will take quite a bit of spray as your practice seat is still close to the falls. However, with continued practice, you can come to appreciate the spectacle from a safe distance; you can still see it vividly, but you aren't constantly sprayed by the falls and you run less risk of falling in.

From this dry station, you can create space and distance between your sense of well-being and the content of your thoughts.

15. Automatic Pilot

Planes can fly themselves and someday soon cars will be able to drive themselves too. But in our own minds, we have already mastered the technology of automatic pilot.

Does this sound familiar? Isn't this how we often live our lives? Haven't you had the experience of driving somewhere and being so engrossed in thinking that you are surprised when you arrive (safely, thankfully) at your destination? This is automatic pilot.

This tendency is an offshoot of adaptive brain mechanisms. As you become expert with something, you relegate the sensory and motor control for the activity to the unconscious. When you were learning to drive or to do some other complex activity, you had to devote considerable conscious attention to it and then, as you became experienced, this attention became automatic. When you develop the expertise to perform the task unconsciously, your mind is freed for imagination, storytelling, and commentary. The challenge then is to bring mindfulness into those activities such as driving, walking, and washing dishes that no longer *require* your conscious attention.

Why bother, you might ask? For one, you spend a good portion of your life doing these mundane activities. If you are awake during these activities, you will simply get more out of life; you will feel more alive, more often. It is also safer to be paying attention. How prepared for an emergency do you think you are while you are driving along unconsciously? How many mistakes have you made and mishaps have you had due to being on automatic pilot?

An example from my own life is the time I injured myself snowboarding while I was having an imaginary conversation in my mind. Interestingly, the snowboarding accident didn't occur on a *steep* slope where my attention was highly focused (with the Fierce Attention of mindfulness) but on an easier slope that I thought didn't require as much attention.

Mindfulness practice can train you to be deliberate and awake. It can develop the skills you need to turn off the automatic pilot to enjoy life—all of life, as it is happening.

16. "Over 400 Channels—For Only $89.95 a Month"

These days, with cable and satellite TV, there are hundreds of channels to choose for your viewing pleasure. With all these choices and a remote control in hand, it's unlikely that you'd sit and watch a bad program—one that is boring, vexing, or makes you feel bad about yourself. Naturally, you would change the channel and surf until you found something more pleasing and entertaining.

And yet, when it comes to our own minds, do we watch some awful programs without changing the channel? Switching channels is the emphasis of cognitive behavioral therapy, where the goal is to exchange maladaptive thoughts (that is, bad TV programs) for adaptive thoughts (that is, good TV programs). With mindfulness, you can become more attuned to the program you are watching and make a choice to switch the channel. You can also make the choice to turn the TV off. You don't need to think all the time!

During one ten-day meditation retreat, my mind was desperate for some kind of stimulation. We were practicing noble silence, which meant no talking, reading, writing, or television while on the retreat. In this stimulation vacuum, I started imagining episodes of the TV program "Cheers." After a while, my mind relented and I started paying attention to what was actually happening.

When you practice mindfulness, notice the mind's tendency toward stimulation and see if it can become fascinated with breathing and feelings in the body instead.

17. Big Mind

Somehow, the experience that comes from meditation feels expansive, bigger, and more spacious. When the mind is spacious, all things can be handled with more ease. The small mind is petty and preoccupied with the needs of the self—it is always asking, "Am I good enough?" "Am I getting enough?" "What are other people thinking of me?" Big mind has the room to go beyond these petty self-concerns and open to the concerns of others.

Mindfulness practice can help to "enlarge" the mind in this way. All that talk and worry in the mind tends to take up less room as the silence of meditation expands our mental space. If we can stop hemming ourselves in with rules, invectives, and "shoulds" then a space can open up. If we stop responding with habitual fear and investing a lot of energy into protecting our small minds, a breathing space can emerge. Mindfulness practice can help to create a space of silence in your life to experience this big mind.

18. Form and Emptiness

Emptiness is a central concept in Buddhism and one that is easily misunderstood. This notion is difficult to translate from the original Sanskrit, *shunyata*. *Shunyata* has also been translated as "void" and this, too, is problematic since it could just as easily be translated as "fullness" or "potential." "Emptiness" may connote blankness or absence and is part of an erroneous image of the Buddha and Buddhists as passionless and apathetic. Emptiness is not empty as in something that was once full and is now used up, like a tank of gas.

Emptiness is a freedom amid the troublesome aspects of mind. Emptiness also refers to the fundamental nature of things. Things are said to be empty of substantial reality, empty of form. This can all be rather confusing, especially when a central Buddhist text, *The Heart Sutra*, proclaims that not only is form emptiness, but emptiness is also form! From this perspective if you attempt to hold on to something that is inherently empty as if it were full, you can only generate misery and suffering.

I like to think of emptiness as that place where nothing extra is added and nothing needs to be removed. Instead you are able to be with whatever is happening no matter what that might be.

With practice, you can move in and out of emptiness and *taste* what it is like. There is peacefulness and calm that comes with tasting emptiness. When you taste emptiness, you will see that most of your distress arises out of what you add to situations.

Metaphors for Self

As with the mind, what we take to be the self can often only be understood in terms of metaphor. Much of how we think of the self is based on what seems self-evident: first and foremost the fact that we *have* a self. Despite this commonsense reality of the self, cognitive science and neuroscience have not located a unified self anywhere in the brain—a finding thoroughly in keeping with ancient empirical observations of the Buddhist tradition. And yet, though there is no cell or brain structure that contains this self, an experience of self nonetheless seems to arise out of the vast and intricate and complex system that is the human mind-body whole.

The *Nova* program "Absolute Zero" helps to elucidate one metaphor for self. In the seventeenth century, "cold" was considered a kind of primordial substance that was "added" to things. Similarly, "heat" was considered an added substance, called *caloric*. The discovery of the laws of thermodynamics later disproved the caloric theory of heat. Likewise, the self is not a substance, a fixed unchanging thing that exists independently of its interconnections. It is a dynamic process that gives the appearance of a substance.

In the Buddhist traditions, there is the notion of buddha-nature. This is the belief that everyone has the capacity to become awakened or enlightened—or depending on the interpretation, that all beings are *already* enlightened even now, but they just don't realize it. In this way, mindfulness does not bring about a particular state of being; it does not "add" enlightenment to unenlightened beings. Rather, it reveals or uncovers what exists already and at the same time reveals the fallacy of a separate and substantial self.

In her lucid and poetic *Buddha*—a retelling of Siddhartha Gautama's life—Karen Armstrong presents the Buddha's view of the self:

> In his view, the more closely we examine ourselves, the harder it becomes to find anything that we can pinpoint as a fixed entity. The human personality was not a static being to which things happened. Put under the microscope of yogic analysis, each person was a process. The Buddha liked to use such metaphors

as a blazing fire or a rushing stream to describe the personality; it had some kind of identity, but was never the same from one moment to another.

If the self is, in this way, essentially metaphorical, it behooves us to understand the metaphors for our experience. Mindfulness meditation practice can help you to dig beneath the surface of the concepts and get closer to life as it is happening, and this can mean cultivating a more fluid and flexible sense of self. In a way, mindfulness is a methodology for developing the capacity for self-observation and for discovering that elusive metaphor for what is me. In fact, you can't spell metaphor without "me!"

It is helpful to make a distinction between the *subject* and the self or selves. The subject is always metaphorically a person and "*exists only in the present.*" The subject is the one who appears to meditate; the one who appears to watch experience and takes note of the activities of the different selves. If you want to know yourself through the process of meditating, then you will increase your access to this *subject* as it sorts through the various configurations of the self.

19. The *Me* Movie

Did you ever notice that the mind makes life into a movie?

As Larry Rosenberg pointed out in a meditation retreat I was attending, this is the *Movie About Me*: starring me, directed by me, produced by me, featuring soundtrack by me, casting by me, screenplay by me—and critiqued and reviewed by me! The mind is the original amateur auteur.

What's more, there is usually plenty of drama (and melodrama) in this feature film and, as the title reflects, a great degree of self-preoccupation. When we live the movie in the first person, we are lost in the mind and not being mindful. When we are able to recognize and watch the movie from some distance away, then we bring mindfulness to life.

The film itself and the wonderful and alluring illusion it creates is also a metaphor for the self. When you watch a movie, you see fluid uninterrupted motion—but it is, of course, just rapid succession of still images or digital pixels. The continuity and fluidity is an illusion courtesy of the nervous system and its sensory apparatus. Likewise, you experience a solid continuous self—this continuity and solidity is an illusion. Consciousness somehow "fills in the gaps" and asserts a continuity of self that neuroscientists—and Buddhists for millennia—say is not there.

Mindfulness practice can help you to identify the elements of this movie and offers the opportunity not to take the self so seriously. Practice helps you to locate gaps in the continuity and to appreciate that this fluidity is an illusion (often a very pleasant one, but still an illusion). You can see in between the individual frames of the film, as it were, and get closer to the dynamic, ever-changing reality of who you really are beyond the illusion.

20. A Flashlight in a Dark Room

The funny thing about consciousness is that it seems to be everywhere. Everywhere you look, it is right there (that is, if you are paying attention!).

But, as the late Julian Jaynes noted:

> Consciousness is a much smaller part of our mental life than we are conscious of, because we cannot be conscious of what we are not conscious of. How simple that is to say; how difficult to appreciate! It is like asking a flashlight in a dark room to search around for something that does not have any light shining upon it. The flashlight, since there is light whatever direction it turns, would have to conclude that there is

light everywhere. And so consciousness
can seem to pervade all mentality when
actually it does not.

So, what's wrong with being a flashlight in a dark
room?

For one thing, it gives a deceptive view of mental
life and the world. It may convince you that your stories are reality itself. When you look out at the world,
you tend to think that this is what the world "really"
looks like. However, it is only how it looks *to you*—a
human animal with eyes and a brain and mind configured in the ways they are configured. How reality
seems to look, how it sounds, and how it feels is all
relative to the system that apprehends it. And losing
sight of this truth is the source of ignorance, arrogance, and self-righteousness to name just few problems. As the perceived center of the universe, we may
easily conclude we are more important—and more
aware—than we actually are.

Mindfulness practice can help you to better know
the nature of consciousness and to become more
clearly aware of its modest and humble scope—
while simultaneously (and somewhat paradoxically)
expanding that scope. Mindfulness practice can be a
helpful antidote to ignorance, arrogance, and righ-
teousness. It can help you to be less invested in being
right for the sake of being right and to be more open
and flexible in your thinking.

And who knows, with continued practice, you may find the light switch that can illuminate the rest of the room.

Perhaps this is the "light" in enlightenment...

21. Witness

Who is it that meditates? Who is it that sometimes is aware of what is happening? Who is it that isn't?

Neither scientists nor philosophers can definitively answer these questions. And yet, there is a part of the mind that watches, witnesses, and observes. Or, as Shunryu Suzuki says in *Zen Mind, Beginner's Mind*, "Your mind is always with the things you observe. So you see, this mind is at the same time everything. True mind is watching mind. Before you see Buddha nature you watch your mind." Mindfulness practice develops the capacity to witness, observe, and spectate on inner and outer events. Mindfulness develops the metaphorical *subject* so that the subject can be more aware of what the metaphorical selves are up to. The ability to witness creates a pause and starts to let a choice be possible. The subject, by knowing the selves, can find the gaps between the impulse to act and the action itself. Think of all the difficulty this might save you: the angry words that aren't spoken, the bag of chips that aren't eaten, the excessive drinks that aren't taken, and the harmful self-judgments that aren't leveled.

What if you were to witness the arising of these impulses without getting sucked into enacting them?

22. "Show Me the Self within the Self"

Just when you think you've figured things out—figured out who you are and how you fit into the world—you discover there is more beneath the surface.

The self is like *matryoshka*, those Russian nesting dolls; there is a smaller version of the figure in each one. Alternatively, think of the image created by two mirrors facing each other; there is an image of the reflection in each reflection—an infinite regress; or, think of peeling away the layers of an onion. This last image is often used particularly in reference to the process of meditation practice. As you go deeper into the self, you find layer after layer. At some point, the onion gives all it has and there is nothing left.

But ultimately, where is that self; where is that *subject* who you call "I"? The nested dolls and the onion do, of course, have a "smallest" or "last" doll or layer—but this is where the metaphor breaks down. Whereas the regressing mirror suggests, perhaps more accurately, that there is no final location for the self.

The Amazing Randi, the renowned parapsychology debunker, has a standing offer to give one million dollars to anyone who can demonstrate, in scientific fashion, a paranormal phenomenon. No one has ever been able to claim this reward. We might just as confidently offer to give a million to anyone who can find the self somewhere inside (or not inside) the brain—and be sure our money was still safe.

Mindfulness practice helps us to see all the productions of the self, layer by layer—and it helps us to not identify with any of the selves as the "final" word on who we are. Practice helps us to see the ephemeral, changing nature of self and to appreciate the process of change itself.

23. Thoughts Like Soap Bubbles

Without mindful awareness, we easily take each thought that arises in our mind for a kind of solid entity that is somehow a definitive truth about reality. But when we look closely at these mental objects, once "solid" or opaque-seeming things reveal themselves to be flimsy and insubstantial, more like a soap bubble than a stone. If you give your full attention to thinking as a process rather than get pulled into the content-story of each thought, the bubble tends to burst. Like soap bubbles, thoughts tend to arise and mindful attention will pop them.

Discovering that your seemingly solid thoughts are flimsy can be of great benefit: it is a first step in breaking your overreliance on and overvaluing of thinking. And when this happens you can also start to see that thoughts are not facts: while thoughts reflect upon or map certain aspects of reality, they are not the last word on reality itself. They are products or constructions of the mind. Indeed, thoughts often can be biased and distorted by your frames of reference, categories, and schemas, and certain kinds of thoughts— like psychotic ones, for instance—can radically depart from reality. For all of us, not just psychotics, being skeptical of thoughts can be healthy. A skeptic is not close-minded. A skeptic says, "Show me the evidence."

The ultimate tricksters are the thoughts that seem to map your individual identity as a solid enduring object. However, this mapping too is comprised of thoughts that arise and burst like soap bubbles. It might seem that something is lost in this conception of the self—but this is not really the case. In fact, if we give up some cherished ideas, these believed thoughts about the self, we start to learn through direct experience the cost of maintaining those ideas. It requires a lot of upkeep, protection, a lot of care and feeding. This so-called solid self is, in fact, the source of a lot of misery.

Yet seeing the insubstantiality of thoughts and beliefs about the self doesn't mean you somehow disappear—you don't disintegrate into nothingness or become unable to function in the world. You don't lose your personality, your passions, interests, or desires. In truth, all you lose is the anxious necessity for things always to go in a particular way.

The experience is often described as liberating, freeing you from all of that anxiety and effort previously dedicated to protecting this solid self. What emerges is closer to who you actually are. You'll be lighter and you'll take yourself less seriously.

24. "Simmer Down"

Imagine a pot on the stove. The pot can be seen as the mind and the self. This is a metaphor for containment and processing.

You can put things in the pot and cook them down. The pot holds them; you can put a lid on it. What is more, by cooking in this way, things are reduced (in the cooking sense of the word). A demi-glaze reduction is cooked for a long time and the result is an intense, flavorful sauce. Things like emotional reactions, impulses, self-deprecation, anxiety, and depression are good candidates to be simmered down.

Cooking makes food digestible and palatable. Likewise cooking your experiences helps to metabolize them. Meditation practice is very much like cooking, especially sitting practice. The sitting posture is stable and contained like the stew pot. While sitting, all manner of intense images, feelings, and thoughts may arise. I find there is sometimes an urge to get off the cushion and go do something else. It is at these moments when something important has arrived that there is great value in staying put and keeping the heat turned on.

Make of yourself a strong pot and put it on the stove. Keep the flame low and steady because you don't want to burn the stew and ruin the pot. Some dishes such as a stew don't require much attending. Just put the ingredients in the pot and let time and the heat do the rest. Other dishes, like risotto, need frequent attention and stirring. It depends on the situation in life. Do you need to be vigilant (during a crisis of some sort) or can you make a slow stew (managing chronic pain, for example)? Put all your concerns and worries in the pot and cook them down slowly. *Bon appétit!*

25. Beasts of Burden

Allowing situations or the opinions and actions of others to determine our self worth is, arguably, a form of insanity. Like oxen pulling a plow, when we yoke our well-being to the vicissitudes of life we are not in control. Mindfulness practice can help us to develop what I call *skeptical noncontingency*. From this place, we skeptically take in all internal and external judgments, endeavoring to be responsive to the feedback of others and situations and at the same time not just buying into anyone else's opinions of us (including our own self-judgments). As well, we endeavor to uncouple or take off the yoke that connects us to the outcomes we cannot control. In this way, circumstances can fluctuate, but our sense of self-value and well-being can remain steady, relatively untouched by the ups and downs of life—our self-value becomes "noncontingent" on the vicissitudes of opinions and circumstance. Equanimity is another hallmark of this approach. When we are equanimous we deal with situations, even difficult ones, with a matter-of-fact form of attention. While difficult situations may be unpleasant, when we have equanimity we have created a space that helps us to cope with the situation without yoking our basic sense of self to outcomes. Equanimity is one of the chief "products" of mindfulness practice because we are learning to be with what is present in the moment with full attention and noncontingent acceptance.

26. Leader of the Pack

Renowned canine behavior expert and "dog whisperer" Cesar Millan recommends the following strategies for establishing a stable, calm, and happy relationship with a dog: exercise, discipline in the form of strong leadership, and affection—in that order.

Our mind is no different. Our thoughts need a calm, stable presence, and a strong leader. In dogs, sometimes the authority of the pack leader may be challenged by another dog fighting for dominance; in the case of our minds, our "strong leadership" is challenged by a troublesome thought or negative belief about ourselves. When this happens, as "pack leader" we can learn to calmly assert our role—our "mindful dominance" and lead attention away from those thoughts and back to the real matter at hand. This is what the "pack leader of the mind" does: it keeps us anchored in the present and redirects us to the present whenever we are not.

You, the *subject*, the witness, and observer can employ the same strategy of exercise, discipline, and affection. Exercise in this case includes physical exercise and mental exercise—specifically mindfulness meditation practice. Discipline is an often misunderstood term that evokes punitive or military images, but in this case, it suggests consistency, effort, and devotion to learning. In fact, etymologically, the word *discipline* is related to the word *disciple* and comes from a Latin word that in fact means "to learn." Discipline is the commitment to learning to take care of yourself in the best way possible. It can also help to give yourself some affection, to adopt a warm attitude toward your imperfections, and to nurture yourself as you work through the exercise and discipline.

Mindfulness practice trains you to become the stable pack leader of your mind. Your doggy mind thoughts will start to happily heel and obey the commands to come, sit, and stay. We can learn to walk the doggy mind instead of being pulled around by it. Good dog!

27. The Finger Pointing to the Moon Is Not the Moon Itself

This traditional Zen image reminds us that we can represent concepts in language just as we can point to the moon—but that representation is not the thing itself. Writing about Buddhism and mindfulness are not the truths that these texts attempt to capture. The truth of our experience lies beyond words.

This could serve as a metaphor for the self when we mistake the concept of the self for the actual moment-by-moment lived energy of the self. The conceptual self looks substantial and solid but it is absent of inherent substance; it's just a representation. Sometimes you may forget that your representation of a thing is not the thing itself. Think about this for a moment. If you are like most people, you have a tendency to live within ideas and concepts, which is like getting caught up in the finger pointing to the moon. You may often be removed from the tangible and dynamic lived experience of things. Alternatively, this is what being in the now has to offer—moving from ideas to direct experience.

The very instructions in mindfulness meditation speak to the difference between representation and the thing itself. When you sit and feel the process of your breathing, it is not the concept of breathing that is noticed, but the actual physical sensations that are present and changing in each moment. You keep returning your attention to these dynamic and tangible sensations. By practicing in this way, it will then be possible to apply this distinction to experiences and events that happen outside of formal meditation practice. These experiences include your job, family, and self. Mindfulness, then, offers a way to get closer to your life, your actual life as it is lived.

28. The Same River

It is said that you can never step in the same river twice.

The self is like a river—constantly changing. The body even changes most of its cells every seven years and nearly all of its atoms annually. A sense of constancy is superimposed over the ceaseless flux of life.

Mindfulness practice helps us recognize a "river of self" as constantly flowing, constantly changing.

Yet, in meditation practice, there is an energetic flow and the astute observer can't help noticing that everything—the river and even the bank—is changing *constantly*. This change is the basic Buddhist principle of impermanence. Experiencing the changing nature of things first hand will help you to identify less with yourself as an unchanging solid entity.

The view of the self as solid and unchanging is, of course, an illusion. However, it is still useful to speak of rivers, such as the Hudson and the Nile, and individual selves, such as you and me, as meaningful entities in the practical world. This doesn't become a problem so long as we understand their changing nature and don't try to cling to them in an unchanging form.

29. Still Forest Pool

In many Buddhist works, the mind and the self are often compared to a pool of water. Thoughts can be seen as a breeze or wind blowing on the surface. These disturbances obscure what can be seen below the surface—the bottom of the pool, the ground of being—without changing it in any way. This ground is there, always there, no matter what is happening on the surface.

If we identify with the surface only, we would have a mistaken view of the self, an incomplete view of reality, and doing so puts us at the mercy of winds and weather—the neverending dramas of daily life. If the wind is calm, and life seems smooth, everything is okay but the moment difficulties arise, the wind is blowing, the "surface-mind" is disturbed, and our clarity compromised. There is wisdom in not locating your sense of well-being at the surface because it frees you from dependence on conditions that you may not be able to control.

Mindfulness practice helps to calm the surface so that you can see ground as well as the surface. Mindfulness also helps to settle the silt at the bottom of the pond when it gets agitated and disturbed. And sometimes, though, mindfulness practice will stir up the bottom of the pond as you work through important issues that may have been ignored or denied for some time before helping you settle back down.

Even the mud is part of the path.

30. "Mirror, Mirror on the Wall"

A flat mirror does not lie. It does not have an opinion. It shows you what you look like in this moment. The mirror is an invitation to meet your self. In a wonderful poem, "Love After Love," Noble Laureate Derek Walcott writes of the happy reuniting of the estranged self with itself: "you will greet yourself arriving / at your own door, in your own mirror."

Sometimes, of course, it can be hard to look into this mirror and to confront what we see. It is particularly hard to look in a mirror if you are feeling bad about yourself, or feeling guilty about something. At other times, we see ourselves just as we are and the result is a smile.

Many spiritual traditions view the student-teacher or guru-disciple relationship in terms of a mirror. The teacher is a mirror for the student, showing the student his or her limitations and potential, reflecting for the student what he or she needs to see right now.

Mindfulness practice helps to develop this sense of welcome mirroring for yourself. Meditation also helps you to develop a capacity for "self-reflection"— in both metaphorical and less metaphorical senses of the word. Mindfulness practice teaches you to look into the mirror of the self without flinching, without running away, and without automatic, blind reaction. It also develops the habit of really seeing what *is* without adornment and without avoidance, without running away and without having a need to get rid of or let go of anything at all.

31. No Taxation without Representation

As every American schoolchild knows, the American Revolutionary War was instigated, in part, because of taxation without representation. The American founders believed this a worthy reason for revolution.

Yet our minds submit, after a fashion, to a different form of "taxation without representation." When our own actions and decisions are not in keeping with our true values, motivations, and highest desires, we are essentially paying tribute to tyranny, giving up letting our true voice be heard—even by ourselves. We our giving up representation in the congress of our own lives.

The founders of the United States did not submit to such injustice and neither should you. Taxes are necessary and they should be fair. The tyrannical self is the inner voice that (like King George III did to the colonies) subjugates others against their self-interest.

But, like the Founding Fathers, you too can challenge the despotic authority of your tyrannical self. This process does not require waging war or, if it is a war, it is one of acceptance, gentleness, and surrender—yielding to present-moment reality as it changes, moment-by-moment, breath-by-breath. Mindfulness practice helps us to identify the tyrannical credos and to recognize the tyrannical self as thoughts and opinions and not as ultimate truth.

Once we learn to recognize the true nature of the tyrants of opinions and judgments, we can expeditiously work to free ourselves from their usurped dominion.

32. Quorum

A dictionary definition of *quorum* is "The minimal number of officers and members of a committee or organization, usually a majority, who must be present for valid transaction of business." One way to think of the self is that it contains multiple selves.

The Tibetan Buddhist teacher Sogyal Rinpoche noted that "we are, at the moment, as if many people all living in one person." Harvard neuroscientist Stephen Pinker echoes this notion when he said, "Our mental life is a noisy parliament of competing factions." Walt Whitman puts it perhaps most succinctly, "I am vast. I contain multitudes."

When thinking of the self, the image of a committee or an executive board requiring a quorum fits nicely. If we act without a quorum, we allow a small and vocal faction of this executive board—a cabal—to take over the business of the self. This faction starts to make decisions based on fear, perfectionism, and unnecessary self-protection, and moves the self toward misery and limitation. We certainly would not want to conduct a business like this, and yet this is exactly how we sometimes end up conducting our lives.

Mindfulness practice helps you to bring all the aspects of the self to the conference table. It allows you to become familiar with the different voices, opinions, and agendas that are present within yourself. It also allows you to choose which of these voices, opinions, and agendas you are going to follow. The quorum is the way to mitigate the worrisome and damaging influence of the tyrannical self.

33. "Put On Your Own Oxygen Mask First"

Many people find it difficult to take care of themselves, often feeling selfish if they attend to their own needs.

Like trying to cut wood with a dull axe, trying to take care of others without taking care of the self first is a counterproductive strategy. The airlines recognize this bit of wisdom. Recall how during the safety announcement, the flight attendant says, "In the event of a loss of cabin pressure, oxygen masks will drop down, and before assisting small children or others, put on your own mask first."

Mindfulness practice is part of the way we can do this. And ultimately, it is only by mindfully caring for ourselves that we can truly and effectively care for others with compassion.

Metaphors for Emotion, Change, and "Ordinary Craziness"

The metaphors in this section delve into the way the mind makes life especially difficult. These metaphors also look at emotions and the process of change. The mind is a creature of habit and often unwilling to give up its cherished routines, even when these routines bring suffering. Modifying our habits is difficult.

Metaphors can be helpful in the process of change by providing an image of how the transformation might take place. In a way, these metaphors can provide a kind of frame—structure, guidance, even comfort. Many of the metaphors in this section deal with the implicit beliefs we have and how these beliefs cause us suffering.

It is hard to separate the mind from what can go wrong with the mind, since so much of what our minds routinely do can be problematic. However, I will take a stab at differentiating "ordinary craziness" from the more troublesome problems of clinical conditions.

34. The Uncertain Fire

Can you embrace the possibility of having what you want? Can you choose what you want instead of all the "shoulds" in your life—the expectations of society, yourself, others, all the ideal and unobtainable self-imposed aspirations for perfection? The idea of choosing what you want and not choosing what you *should* want also includes embracing or managing your basic responsibilities. These competing sources can be confusing; this confusion can burn like a fire. This fire is scary and potentially dangerous, so it needs containment, and of course you don't want the conflagration of a spreading wildfire on your hands. Mindfulness provides the containment for that fire.

Mindfulness practice will help to give you ready access to the important information your feelings hold while at the same time helping you not get sucked wholly into or dominated by them. In fact, the basic approach to mindfulness is to move attention to these feelings in the body and to keep returning attention to them whenever attention moves away. Such back and forth movement of attention fosters intimacy and connection with the body, a true sense of what is important to you, beyond all the *shoulds*.

Mindfulness itself can also be thought of as a fire that consumes the irrelevant and the unnecessary. Burning like a bonfire, you can move toward freedom and burn everything else away without a trace.

Shunryu Suzuki puts it like this:

> In order not to leave any traces, when you do something, you should do it with your whole body and mind; you should be concentrated on what you do. [D]o it completely, like a good bonfire, […]not a smoky fire. [B]urn yourself completely. If you do not burn yourself completely, a trace of yourself will be left in what you do. You will have something remaining which is not completely burned out. Zen activity is activity which is completely burned out, with nothing remaining but ashes.

35. The Man Trap

An episode aired during the first season of the original *Star Trek* series titled the "The Man Trap" provides a vivid portrayal of the power of denial.

In this episode, Dr. McCoy encounters an old girlfriend, Nancy. To him she looks like the young woman he knew years ago. To another crewmember she looks like a woman he met once on a pleasure planet. The hapless and expendable crewmember (a Redshirt) goes off with her and, predictably, winds up dead—all the salt sucked out of his body. Later we discover that "Nancy" actually is a being that can change forms and who requires massive quantities of salt to survive, which the shapeshifting creature gets by sucking it out of the blood of humans. At the dramatic peak of the episode, Dr. McCoy must kill "Nancy" in order to save Captain Kirk's life. He knows at an intellectual level that Nancy is a murderous creature, however in his heart he cannot accept it. He cannot believe something other than what his eyes tell him. Fortunately for the Captain, he shakes himself out of his denial, much like coming out of a trance, and he fires his phaser at the creature.

How often do you engage in situations like Dr. McCoy where you know something to be the case yet you cannot fully acknowledge it because you wish so fervently for it to be different? Perhaps it is a relationship you know to be unhealthy, yet you cannot leave it. You want or need to see your partner in a certain way, regardless of the way that person actually is. You may get burned and burned again, yet attachment persists.

To the extent that mindfulness practice helps you to perceive reality in the moment more clearly, it can help you to have clearer contact with that reality. Mindfulness can help you to move toward perception that is more accurate, less clouded by desire and denial. It can help you to develop more trust in what you perceive because you have practiced paying very close attention to what you feel in the body in the moment. It can help you to make contact with the wisdom of your feelings and to be better equipped to deal with the thought-creations of your desirous and wistful mind.

Mindfulness helps ground head, heart, and "Bones" in what actually is.

36. Emotional Baggage

Imagine a big sack that you carry around with you at all times. Into that sack goes everything you are holding on to—every disappointment, trauma, and wrong you've ever experienced. You can imagine that sack might get heavy. This image, the metaphor of emotional baggage, has penetrated our culture.

How many times have you heard in a movie, on television, or from a friend that "she's got baggage"? Or "he's carrying a lot from childhood"? How much time and energy are taken up by what you are carrying? How much of your emotional energy is spent hauling your baggage and fighting to keep it tightly closed, holding heavy memories and beliefs out of awareness?

Mindfulness practice can help you to identify, set down, and unload this baggage. The first step, of course, is simply to notice and really feel the weight of your heavy burden: ancient stories and beliefs about yourself and the world, hardened judgments, childhood hurts. Meditation practice will help this to happen. And when it does, you have the opportunity to really *look* at it instead of stuffing it away and dragging it along. By taking the step of identifying and looking at the baggage, you have the opportunity to unpack all those stored experiences—perhaps saving the ones that are valuable and "donating" the rest to charity.

Think about what you could do with all that extra energy once it is freed from carrying around those emotional bags! Imagine how light you would feel!

37. Guardianship of Solitude

The poet Rainer Maria Rilke offered the metaphor of the guardian for serious relationships in his "Letters on Love":

It is a question in marriage, to my feeling, not of creating a quick community of spirit by tearing down and destroying all boundaries, but rather a good marriage is that in which each appoints the other guardian of his solitude and shows him this confidence, the greatest in his power to bestow. A *togetherness* between two people is an impossibility, and where it seems, nevertheless, to exist, it is a narrowing, a reciprocal agreement which robs either one party or both of his fullest freedom and development. But, once the realization is accepted that even between the *closest* human beings infinite distances continue to exist, a wonderful living side by side can grow up, if they succeed in loving the distance between them which makes it possible for each to see the other whole and against a wide sky!

How can you be simultaneously yourself and with another?

Rilke wrote this long before there were family therapists, yet he describes what they would characterize as fusion and recommends an autonomous, mature path in relationships. The challenge of the mature relationship is to neither subvert nor impose the self on the intimate other.

Mindfulness in a relationship is the most challenging and fruitful place to apply the practice. Intimate relationships also provide the greatest opportunity to see where your buttons are and how they work when they are pushed. Interpersonal interactions are often difficult and complex, and may be the place we are most prone to be mindless and reactive.

38. "Perfectomy"

One time a few years ago, I was teaching an Introduction to Psychology class at a time when I was also working with a patient who struggles with obsessive-compulsive disorder (OCD), wherein she had compulsive needs to do all things perfectly. Part of what I was teaching was the history of the treatment of mental disorders, and part of this gruesome history is the once-common practice of lobotomy, a surgical removal or destruction of parts of the brain. As I reflected to my patient that the need to be perfect can be woven into the very fabric of the self, become part of every thought, and inform every feeling that you might have, these two ideas bumped into each other and I imagined a procedure that might be called a "perfectomy."

But unlike the ill-advised lobotomies of the 1950s, a *perfectomy* is performed with mindfulness, a non-surgical, non-invasive, and safe procedure that helps you to identify and ameliorate perfectionistic tendencies. Mindfulness accomplishes this by letting you become more intimate with your own mind, by bringing conscious attention to realms of thought and feeling that had been operating unnoticed under automatic control. Mindfulness also helps you to identify major themes in perfectionism and to greet these themes with gentleness and curiosity rather than compulsive, reflexive responses.

39. In a Hole with a Shovel

Imagine you are in a ditch or down in a hole. The only tool you have is a shovel, and so you try to use the shovel to dig yourself out of the hole. Of course, this will never work: you dig furiously for hours, days, and weeks, but you only get deeper into the hole.

How often do we do some version of this in our lives?

Because we are addicted to thinking, we tend to rely on thinking first, sometimes even believe it is the only tool we own. When the storytelling mind has created suffering for us, using more stories, more thinking, to get free from suffering is like using a shovel to get out of a hole.

The body is the way out of rumination, and mindfulness of the body and its sensations is a tool we always have on hand.

40. Deprivation Mind

The meditation teacher Ram Dass uses the term "Deprivation Model"—and I'd like to offer a slight variant: the deprivation *mind*. The deprivation mind is a particular version of the storytelling mind. The deprivation mind is always looking at the world and saying, "I don't have enough"—whether it be enough love, sex, money, comfort, ease, recognition, validation, understanding, security, or any of a host of similar such things. The deprivation mind is especially prone to catastrophizing about a future that won't have enough of whatever the mind is preoccupied with or a future in which whatever it does have is lost. The deprivation mind can be a subtle yet pervasively destructive force in life.

Deprivation mind can also contribute to case-building for the fact that you are deficient or defective in some way. Of course it's the case that if you are inundated with the internal or external message that you don't have enough, you can easily come to believe there is something wrong with you, and that having more of *something* would fix it—and you can thank Madison Avenue and our consumer culture for some of this.

A cartoon in *The New Yorker* published after the start of the Iraq war shows an Iraqi man standing on bomb-strewn ground wearing an "I love USA" T-shirt.

Over the caption "Liberated Iraqi," this man is having the following thoughts: "Am I losing my hair?" "Am I gaining too much weight?" "Is my breath O.K.?" "Are my teeth white enough?" "Do I need a new car?" "Is my deodorant letting me down?" This is the deprivation mind in action.

And yet, everything is of the nature to change; this is the truth of impermanence. But impermanence need not be deprivation. When you can mindfully sit and actually be present to and experience the changing nature of life, moment-by-moment, you can start to see the practical wisdom of not trying to grasp after things and not trying to push things away.

Mindfulness practice will help acquaint you with your deprivation mind, and its cousins deficiency mind and defective mind. It will show you the places where your storytelling mind is actively complaining about what it thinks it does not have in sufficient quantity or what is wrong with you or your life. By exchanging the habit of complaining with the habit of mindful attention, you can move away from the "ordinary craziness" of these minds and closer toward acceptance and satisfaction.

41. "I've Got Good News and I've Got Bad News"

Let's start with the good news. The human body has a remarkable and sophisticated set of systems designed to cope with stress. These systems include the brain, autonomic nervous, endocrine, and immune systems. They work in precise, capable, and efficient coordination with one another to maintain complex levels of balance and support adaptation in threatening and dangerous situations. Remarkable. That's the good news.

Now for the bad news: You were born about 100,000 years too late for these systems to work exactly right for you. These processes evolved in the environment of our human ancestors as a response to acute stressors. The body-mind releases a vast amount of energy to cope with a stressful situation. It pumps the brain and body full of neurotransmitters and neurohormones to mobilize action. This is the notorious fight-or-flight response. These systems were not designed for chronic stressors such as traffic, overcrowding, difficult bosses, financial worries, conflicted marriages, and information overload. In fact, this "legacy brain" saw few of the conditions we confront today.

The legacy brain's purpose is to keep you safe and intact—to protect you from a dangerous environment replete with predators, starvation, freezing, and social threats. And the legacy brain is biased toward anxiety. Think about this. Evolution proceeds by survival of the fittest—but fittest does not necessarily mean the strongest or most intelligent, as is often misunderstood—but rather, the fittest are those most responsive to change who live long enough to have reproductive success and pass along their genes to the next generation. In a dangerous environment, those who were most vigilant and attuned to potential danger would be most likely to survive. This is why negative feelings are more common, remembered better, and more potent—because they helped early humans to adapt. This negativity bias makes sense because the cost of guessing wrong (e.g., "Was that really a tiger? Eh, I guess I won't worry about it.") could be dreadfully high.

Understanding what the stress response system evolved to do can be especially helpful. Mindfulness practice can help you to get familiar with the way stress feels in the body: a tightness in the chest, a flushed face, the heart pounding, the sound of rushing blood in the ears, a clenching fist. At times, you may be so engrossed in thoughts and stories that these feelings might be your first clue that you are stressed or anxious. This awareness can prompt you to extricate yourself from the dramatic storyline of your thoughts and to return to the present.

42. The Drama Sutra

Are you "addicted" to commotion, theater, and spectacle? How much chaos is there in your life? How much of this chaos may be elective or avoidable? Are you "addicted" to commotion and drama? When we act on automatic pilot, we typically act in ways that increase drama, not decrease it.

Mindfulness practice helps to overcome this tendency to act out in ways that create more and more endless drama in our lives and to bring our attention to the whole of our lives, without letting the Drama Sutra dominate center stage.

The prelude to the Drama Sutra will have characteristic feeling signatures in the body. These will become familiar with mindfulness practice. By focusing on the body instead of on the story, you deprive the Drama Sutra of its driving force. Storytelling mind thinking sustains the Drama Sutra. Instead of dwelling on the social drama, focus instead on the wonderful and intricate internal drama of how experience changes moment by moment. If you can be fascinated by the present experience, you'll have less interest in creating the Drama Sutra—and also less interest in watching all of its rehearsals and performances!

43. "Don't Believe Everything You Think"

We've all been admonished not to believe everything we read—after all, the press is fallible and marketers are always selling you something. The best approach to the written word is to develop a healthy skepticism. But what about the *cogitated* word?

I've seen a bumper sticker that neatly sums it up for us: "Don't Believe Everything You Think." Perhaps this slogan can be updated to "Don't Believe *Anything* You Think," at least not without a skeptical review.

If we validate thoughts as truths simply because they originate within our own skull we're going to generate misery. What might it mean to recognize thoughts as just thoughts and develop a healthy skepticism toward them, without mistaking our thoughts for ultimate truths? Is there a way to do this without becoming cynical or debilitated?

We can start with the thoughts that have a negative flavoring, the ones that are critical in nature. When they arise, first ask, "Is there any important feedback for me here; is there something for me to learn?" If so, identify that important feedback, say "Thank you" to the critical thought, and move on, integrating that feedback to the extent that it is useful and possible. Often, however, there is no useful feedback or corrective action to take, such as when you are dealing with a generalized criticism like, "I am no good."

Mindfulness practice will help you to become "suspicious" of these thoughts and less sucked into their negativistic stories. It takes some practice and time to develop the sensitivity to recognize the feeling flavor of the tyrannical self—the inner voice screaming thoughts and hawking them as the final words on all matters.

With mindfulness practice, you can bring a degree of distance and incredulity to such interior utterances. You can smile and ask patiently, "Says who?"

44. "Ninety Miles an Hour Is the Speed I Drive"

A car driven at high speed is a dangerous object. For this reason, people must be licensed to drive and many laws, such as speed limits, govern their behavior in cars. The mind, speeding at breakneck velocities from place to place, can also be a dangerous force—and unfortunately, there is no license to obtain and no laws governing its private behavior. Though much has been written, in Buddhist sources and other places, about suggestions for the safe and nonharming usage of the mind.

No sensible person would drive a racecar without appropriate training—but what about the racing mind? Mindfulness practice is kind of like "driver's ed" for the mind. Mindfulness practice will show you how to handle thoughts; to see thoughts as objects instead of as reality itself; and to see thoughts as productions of the mind that can be fallible, gullible, and credulous.

We can even extend this vehicular metaphor a little further: the overheating engine of the car is the body's stress response, and chronic stress is akin to the engine idling at a too-high speed. It's not good for an engine and can wear out your body too. And the overlearned habit of stress and its attendant neurohormones and physiological arousal are like driving the car at high speeds. Even if you could manage to drive safely down certain stretches of the highway at 90 mph, when you let your foot off the gas, the car does not stop right away, nor does the feeling of motion—the car can coast unsafely for a great distance, or the sharp turn or stopped car in front of you could come up way too hard and fast. The body's physiological stress response doesn't instantly dissipate when the crisis is over or the deadline is met. Even when we "turn off" the stress response systems or take our foot off the gas, we still have to metabolize all those neurohormones. And that often feels in the body like anxiety.

With mindfulness, you can take that anxious, panicked "sense of speed" as an object of meditation by sitting down and really noticing how it feels in the body. Moreover, make sure that you do this while resisting the temptation to get involved and make stories about these feelings.

It takes time for the adrenaline and other hormones to be metabolized. Likewise, when you are anxious for whatever reason, knowing what is happening in the body and paying attention to the feelings themselves (instead of the meanings or stories) helps to keep you from compounding the stress physiology into anxiety and distress.

45. "Man Loses Arm in Tragic Industrial Accident"

Occasionally, there is a story in the news of a tragic industrial accident. A worker gets too close to the machinery and his or her shirt gets caught in the works. The machine pulls in the shirt and then flesh and bone with a grisly outcome.

The mind can work much like this. The mind can latch on to some idea or situation—a momentary difficulty or setback, an unkind remark from colleague or friend—and, before you know it, your entire self has been pulled into the works and is being mangled. The mind tends to elaborate, amplify, and magnify small things through the dangerous "machinery" of rumination, regret, and worry.

Mindfulness practice can help you to disengage attention before things get too ugly. With continued practice, it can help you to avoid wearing long blousy shirtsleeves too close to the hungry machinery of the storytelling mind. It also helps to develop precision of mind and vigilant attention—the proper "protective eyewear" and "safe workplace procedures"—that can help keep you free from the devastating effects of your mental machinery.

46. Don't Give the Bully Your Lunch Money

Certain factions of the mind can be bullies.

Consider this image: You are on your way to school whistling and happy and, all of a sudden, the school bully corners you. He towers over you and demands your lunch money. Intimidated, fearful for your physical safety, you fork it over. Little do you know, this bully is actually a scared little boy himself, and if you were to stand up to him, he'd back down.

The bullies of the mind are like this too: insubstantial, not a real threat, and willing to back down when challenged. But, like many bullies, the ones in the mind "count on" the expectation that you will back down, that you'll capitulate without resistance or investigation.

Of course, the arrival of the bully is unpleasant, to be sure. It may be accompanied by intense feelings of anxiety. The bully may say terrible things. He may threaten harm, even mortal injury. But don't yield. Instead, create a space for the mental bully to occupy.

Don't get caught up in the stories, images, and feelings the bullying thoughts present. Notice how the body feels instead of stories about what the body feels (for example, "Oh interesting, look how my stomach is fluttering"). Don't elaborate those sensations into stories. Stay as close to the body as you can.

And just as with school bullies, the more you give in to your own bullying thoughts the more powerful they become, just as anxiety grows more consuming when you give in to its conditions. For example, if you fear something and always avoid what you fear, anxiety is reinforced. By not testing the truth of the anxiety, you never find out that there is no real danger. Likewise, if you always give the bully your lunch money, you'll never find out what happens if you don't. What would happen if you confronted him? You may just find out there is nothing substantial here—nothing that presents an actual threat to your physical or psychological integrity.

You can also practice *compassion* for this bully who feels he must threaten and terrorize in order to feel whole; and you can practice steadying compassion for yourself even as fearful thoughts arise. And, of course, even just by extending compassion to the bully, you are really extending compassion to yourself. And perhaps unlike school bullies, bullying thoughts often come from a misguided attempt to protect you.

But be careful: resistance to the bully does not mean fighting violence with violence, but rather a patient, equanimous challenge to the validity of the bully. By welcoming and owning the bully, you can eliminate the struggle, the hardship, and the self-judgment that can accompany his demands.

The bully is, after all, part of the self.

And now you can enjoy your lunch!

47. Spaz

A muscle spasm can be a painful and distressing experience. Not enough stretching or hydration and too much use may cause the spasm. Like muscle spasms, you have probably experienced your share of psychological spasms. Taking a cue from the language of schoolkids, I simply refer to this as *spazzing*. Like a muscle that may be out of condition and not ready for the load placed on it, the mind can also be out of shape and readily go into a spasm.

The occurrence of an unexpected or bizarre thought may send the mind into a "spasm." The appearance of the thought sets in motion a cascade of other events, which are reactions to the triggering thought. These reactions complicate, compound, and amplify the original event. Throw in a robust dose of self-judgment, self-loathing, and self-deprecation and the mind will tighten itself into painful "spasticity."

Mindfulness practice is the equivalent of gentle stretching and exercise for the mind, making it nimble, responsive; it provides plenty of "hydration," letting the mind be ready for exertion without going into spastic waves of energy. Mindfulness also helps to counteract and avert the amplification process.

Sometimes spasms are unavoidable. Yet how differently we respond to the mental kind than the merely physical. After all, if you had a case of bursitis that was sending your shoulder into frequent spasms, you probably would not be making a case against yourself for how awful a person you are. However, if your *mind* goes into spasm over something you have said or done, you just might make this case against yourself.

Mindfulness helps you to be less judgmental and more equanimous toward your experience.

48. Thirty-One Emotional Flavors

Just as Baskin-Robbins used to advertise thirty-one flavors of ice cream, the body has a multitude of "flavors" to its embodied feelings. These feelings are a repository of information, knowledge, and wisdom. These feelings reflect your responses to the world and can sometimes (but not always!) tell you, if you can listen, important information about what you need to know and where you need to go. And yet, as we've seen above, they are not themselves ultimate truths.

Nonetheless our feeling system is a vast and vital resource. How do we discern feelings with real and useful information from feelings with no useful content? The useful feelings are based on direct and accurate information. Less useful ones tend to be based on distortions or rule-bound thoughts that are not consistent with our true desires. For example, negative self-judgment has a particular feeling "flavor." After practicing mindfulness, you'll become familiar with this feeling flavor, and by doing so be less prone to believe the negative view. We can recognize it more readily, "Ah, self-judgment," and move on.

Mindfulness can help you to gain access to and become familiar with this feeling system without being compulsively bound to it. Mindfulness will help you to connect with the wisdom, knowledge, and information that reside in the body in every moment. And as we've repeatedly seen, meditation practice itself is focused in large part on the feelings in the body and can be effective in connecting with your "gut sense," and knowing what you truly want to do.

49. "Burn, Baby, Burn"

The feelings that come with "ordinary craziness"— fears and worries, grasping wants and conditioned aversion, and even the "extraordinary" kind, like depression—are practically impossible without stories about a past or a future. Indeed, our relationship to time is implicated in a vast majority of human suffering and misery, especially anxiety and depression.

A fire cannot burn in a vacuum because there is no oxygen. In this metaphor, the present moment is like a vacuum chamber; anxiety, like fire, requires oxygen to burn. There is plenty of oxygen in the past and the future, and anxiety burns bright. If we remain in the present moment, what can burn? Anxiety cannot be sustained solely by the present.

Take regret and worry, the prize products of the past and future. Regret is rich in oxygen. Do you sometimes repeat the same thing over and over again? The first couple of times you do this there may be important information gleaned in the process. In other words, "I learned something from that situation that I will take into account and I won't make the same mistake again." But thoughts are rarely so practical. When you ruminate, the mind goes far past the point of diminishing returns. Likewise, worry, the scion of the future, may contain some valuable and important information to help you plan. However, after the seventeenth time going over some prospect in the future, checking your watch repeatedly, and rehearsing the same scenes in the mind repetitively, you're needlessly expending energy, creating more anguish for yourself. The mind becomes preoccupied with a morbid future, full of bleak outcomes and dire happenings. Depression thrives in this atmosphere. Depression may recruit the past as evidence for the defectiveness or unworthiness of the self.

Mindfulness practice helps you to create a vacuum chamber and keep it airtight. Awareness of the present moment is this vacuum chamber, and returning over and over to the present, just as it is, is the way to keep the chamber sealed. With continued practice, this vacuum can become stable and accessible, readily available whenever the mind has ventured into the territory of regret or worry.

50. Cleopatra Syndrome

I'm not here, this isn't happening.

There's an old joke that asks, "Why couldn't Cleopatra ever accept the truth?" and then delivers the punchline: "Because she was the Queen of *DE-NILE*." [*Insert drum sting here*. Thank you very much—I'm here all week. Please tip your waitresses.]

Denial is, of course, one of the many defense mechanisms at our disposal—albeit one of the most costly ones. It's true that sometimes we need to put some fact or crisis temporarily out of our mind to focus on a difficult or urgent task at hand, but full-blown denial is rarely helpful. And when denial becomes a way of life, an inflexible conditioned response to life's challenges, we are often digging ourselves in deeper. This way of life could be called "the Cleopatra Syndrome."

The paradox of mindfulness is that it encourages you to move *toward* scary or difficult situations instead of away from them. In this way, it can be a potent antidote to the Cleopatra Syndrome. Mindfulness is a tool that allows you to look at yourself with an intimate and receptive eye, to really see, in all its starkness, the reality of your life. At times, this can seem overwhelming, and sometimes when people first start to practice mindfulness they feel like they may have actually become *more* anxious since they started practicing. (Playing on this, when I teach Mindfulness-Based Stress Reduction, I joke that there is a small typo in the brochure, and welcome everyone to their first "Stress *Induction*" class. It's usually good for a chuckle.)

But even if you have experiences that seem overwhelming when you sit down to meditate, stick with it. If you do, soon you'll be the one in charge of your life—and not the Queen of Denial!

51. "Please Pass the Tums"

In Charles Dickens' *A Christmas Carol*, when Scrooge is confronted by the ghost of his old business partner, Jacob Marley, Scrooge thinks the ghost can't possibly be real. "Why do you doubt your senses?" Marley asks. And Scrooge replies:

> Because... a little thing affects them. A slight disorder of the stomach makes them cheats. You may be an undigested bit of beef, a blot of mustard, a crumb of cheese, a fragment of an underdone

potato. There's more of gravy than of grave about you, whatever you are!

Like Scrooge's "bit of beef" and "blot of mustard" some experiences remain undigested and stuck in the craw of the mind, where they can cause all kinds of danger, big and small. When it is a traumatic or stressful experience, these experiences can be reexperienced and repeated, coming "back up" as if you have indigestion. Sometimes, it can feel like "acid reflux of the mind"—a painful reliving of the original distress or sometimes even just a by-product of a "mental digestive system" that isn't working quite right. Mindfulness practice can help you to metabolize and digest past experiences, and "neutralize" the acid of a painful experience.

To get a sense of how this works, consider that in general and simplified terms, when thoughts arise in the mind you have one of three choices of what to do in response: ignore, identify, or "*dis*identify." Ignoring can be effective at reducing momentary distress but it does not help to metabolize or digest a traumatic past or a difficult event. It may also be an "expensive" way to cope because avoidance behaviors almost always eat up time and energy that could be spent more productively elsewhere. The second option is to identify yourself wholly with the traumatic past and with the storytelling mind's stories about that past. And when you identify with the stories, you recreate the experience as if the trauma were happening now.

For instance, you know the storytelling mind is active if you are saying things like, "Look how this ruined my life and is continuing to ruin my life; I'll never be whole again; I feel worthless and damaged." There is often a component of self-blame—a double victimization—"I shouldn't have let this happen to me; what's wrong with me?" When identification occurs the trauma is refreshed and even strengthened. Trauma is a remarkably resilient phenomenon.

The third option is "disidentifying" with the thought, which is just a word that means recognizing that the thought is a thought without identifying yourself wholly with it—and this is where mindfulness becomes helpful and therapeutic. When the traumatic material arises and presents itself to the mind, you acknowledge it and then step back, creating a safe distance from which to watch the scene unfold. You can watch the scene without elaborating or embellishing it in any way. It can be helpful to remind yourself that the past is not happening now, especially when the memories are vivid and activate the physiological symptoms of the stress response system.

Each time you greet the past from this place of disidentification, a bit of it is digested and metabolized—getting from it what is "nutritious" and valuable, and "excreting" or processing the rest. As a trauma is metabolized, you will gradually become less and less distressed and less and less identified with and controlled by the traumatic or stressful past. The memories are not eradicated by disidentification, of course, but their emotional impact is diminished—they'll cause less indigestion, fewer painful hallucinations. We can also name this "befriending" painful thoughts. Befriending those thoughts changes your relationship to them in a wholesome way. And disidentification helps you to overcome feelings of self-blame that may accompany a troubled past.

52. "Shoot First, Ask Questions Later"

Our brains are built in ways that facilitated the survival of our early human ancestors. As I've mentioned before, we all have a "legacy brain"—a brain adapted to the world of 100,000 years ago and, unfortunately, not particularly optimized for the demands of today. In the legacy environment, survival was paramount and one of the most important set of functions of the human brain was predicting, detecting, and responding to or avoiding mortal danger. In short, the legacy brain was always alert to threat, always ready at an instant's notice to activate the set of responses—including behavioral reactions like "fight or flight" and the chemical and hormonal responses that cause, for instance, an increased heart rate or emotional states like anger or fear. This set of reactions makes up the stress response system.

Activating the stress response system to a potential but not yet actual danger is costly in terms of the time and calories expended, but far less costly than being attacked by a tiger—and so we are designed to err on the side of caution, becoming "protectively" stressed even when no real stressor, no genuine threat, is in fact present. The limbic system of the brain is primarily involved in this threat response system. It is an older part of the brain also known as the "emotional" brain. We share these structures with all mammals; there is nothing uniquely human about its structure or function. (The "human part" comes into play with the frontal lobes of the cerebral cortex, which are primarily involved in "executive" functions like planning and decision-making, and are disproportionately larger in humans relative to other animals.)

One structure in the limbic system, the amygdala, is worth getting to know by name. This structure is in many ways responsible for our emotional reactions to threat and danger (among other things). It is responsible for the near instantaneous activation of potentially life-saving responses (in the legacy environment, remember!) like fear and anger. If the amygdala is overly reactive, there can be issues such as panic disorder or rage responses, where the brain and body's threat response system is being turned on for little or no apparent reason. In a very real way, the limbic system of the legacy brain is hardwired to "shoot first" and only later does the cortex of the frontal lobes show up to "ask questions" about what may or may not be dangerous in this particular situation.

Mindfulness practice can help you to "talk back" to the limbic system before it takes control of your behavior. It can help you to discern and discriminate between situations that hold actual threat from those that are false alarms. Mindfulness practice can also help you to become more comfortable with the neurochemical and neurohormonal products of the limbic system and the stress response system. With this comfort, you can recognize how adrenaline feels and how it affects the body and notice when its effects are present without necessarily "believing" the "story" of fear that those chemicals seem to tell. You won't be forced to interpret these bodily feelings in a fearful way that compounds the situation.

In short, mindfulness practice can help you "ask questions first" and only "shoot" when absolutely necessary. What's more, it can actually help you to *reduce* the number of situations where this decision *is* necessary.

53. Quack, Quack, Quack

Remember the animated versions of Charles Schulz's *Peanuts* cartoons? The voices of adults were always represented by a muted and somewhat off-key slide trombone. And this always sounded to me like a kind of squawking, or maybe the honking chatter of quacking ducks (*"Quackquack quaquackquack quack"*).

It can often be valuable to practice "hearing" verbal productions as just this kind of squawking or quacking—especially the ones inside our own head. How rarely is there any really useful information there, and how often is it just that much noise! In fact, I'm willing to venture that verbal productions of one kind or another trigger much of your distress. I'm sure you've had the experience of being on the telephone with someone who was going on and on and in frustration you've held the phone away from your ear as the person blathers on, attending to something more useful or interesting. If you can learn to do this with *your own* thoughts—the ruminative, nonproductive, strident thoughts—it can be of great benefit. It can be really helpful to imagine replacing the endless elaborate scripts, stories, and implications of the communication with a simple quacking, "Oh there goes my mind again: *Quackquack quaquackquack quack*." If you can do this, even a little, you will reduce or eliminate a lot of suffering.

Mindfulness practice can help you to see the mind in this perspective, to see the mind's productions as not always being all equally worthy of attention. Of course, you must still distinguish thoughts that need your attention from those that are junk and it is often the case that other people occasionally do have important information or feedback for us—but by and large, you don't need to get caught up in the stories and implications.

Enjoy the quacking!

54. The Hornet's Nest

Imagine you are walking along a path toward an important destination. The path is narrow and one point enters a tunnel—and inside the tunnel there is a hornets' nest. You have no choice but to go right by the nest, potentially disturbing the hornets and becoming the object of their fury. But there's no other way.

The hornets' nest is a metaphor for being stuck in an unavoidably difficult situation, perhaps a troubling relationship, for example. So often, we tend to avoid confronting what needs to be confronted for fear of the pain that the hornets will cause and, thus, we remain stuck, trapped, unable to get where we need to go.

Mindfulness practice may occasionally bring you into close proximity of a hornets' nest. The hornets may attack, and many things you've been avoiding or trying to stay away from may now be experienced. Things may feel worse before they feel better. It is important to persist with practice and to work with whatever comes up during life and meditation with curiosity and gentleness. And you'll eventually be past the hornet's nest, getting on with your life.

Once these previously avoided things are dealt with, you will experience a measure of freedom and maybe even change. As the saying goes, the only way beyond is through. The way to overcome something is not to avoid it, but to move into it.

55. The Investing Dentist

How can we tell the difference between meaningful thoughts and those that are random and unproductive?

Nassim Taleb, a professional stock trader and mathematics professor who writes on the cognitive aspects of economics, illustrates this point with an investing example: He invents a retired dentist who is a successful investor. This dentist expects to have a 93% probability of making money in a given year. The dentist plans to take advantage of his free time by monitoring his stock prices closely. Is this a wise strategy for him? Assuming his monitoring will not change the outcome, the wisdom of this action comes in seeing the types of feelings he experiences as he checks his investments. Given the parameters of his investments and their probabilities, Taleb is able to calculate the probability of whether the dentist is making or losing money at any given moment of observation. For instance, if he checks his stock prices every second (which is essentially possible now with available technology) there is only a 50.02% probability that he will be making money at that precise moment. Unfortunately, Taleb says, the dentist does not have a hearty emotional constitution: "He feels a pang with every loss, as it shows in red on his screen. He feels some pleasure when the performance is positive, but not in equivalent amount as the pain experienced when the performance is negative." By this analysis, the dentist gets only 241 pleasant moments for every 239 unpleasant moments each day and winds up emotionally exhausted. However, if he were to change his strategy to a monthly check-in, there is a 67% chance that he will be making money and the ratio of pangs to pleasure will be 1:2 (instead of nearly 1:1 with continuous checking). In this hypothetical investing example, there is a known ratio of noise to meaningful indications of performance.

Similarly, it can sometimes be counterproductive to over-evaluate the global state of one's life. The storytelling mind is easily fooled by random variation, and quickly jumps into stories about what each uptick or downtick "means."

What to do then with variability? In any given moment, you will be subject to variability—the state of your body (tired, hungry, sleepy, achy, itchy, relaxed, energized, and so forth), the state of your surroundings (hot, cold, comfortable, uncomfortable, and so forth), and your state of feelings (confident, certain, tentative, expanding, contracting, and so forth). We can use meditation to let the noise settle. And moreover, we can actually take the *variation itself* as a focus of the meditation, just noticing and watching the vicissitudes of body and mind without interpretation, judgment, and story.

56. "Might as Well Face It, You're Addicted to Thoughts"

We often hear of addiction to alcohol, smoking, drugs, gambling, sex, and the Internet—but outside of some Buddhist publications, we don't hear much about addiction to *thoughts*. Thinking accompanies just about every activity that we engage in—taking a shower, washing the dishes, driving, walking, working, and so on. There are few circumstances where we are not thinking. Aside from deliberate thinking, such as planning, problem solving, analyzing, and being creative, most of the thinking that we engage in is automatic and discursive—a product of the storytelling mind. It has little utility and often actually distracts us from more useful ways to use our mind and our life. And yet we do it anyway. It is, quite literally, a kind of addiction.

This addiction is so pervasive and so seamless that we probably don't even think about the fact that we are thinking all the time. We may not realize we are addicted. And moreover we come to interpret our addiction as a *good thing*, overvaluing, even prizing it. Why would we want to give that up?

One of the first discoveries you might make while sitting down to meditate is how busy the mind is. The simple instruction of paying attention to the breath will reveal this. The meditation teacher Chögyam Trungpa Rinpoche spoke about "The great collection of things in one's mind." This is what you have to contend with when you try to meditate. You might often try to think yourself out of a problem that thinking got you into in the first place. Thinking begets more thinking.

Sometimes, though, the key is to not talk to yourself but instead, drop into silence and notice what that feels like.

57. "No One Told Me the War Was Over"

In "The Emissary," an episode of *Star Trek: The Next Generation*, the Enterprise encounters an old Klingon vessel, the T'Ong, whose crew has been in sleep stasis for a century. In the original series, the Federation and the Klingons were at war. In the *Next Generation*, the Federation and Klingons are allies. Unfortunately, the Klingon crew in stasis does not know this and are not likely to believe that things have changed. They are about to wake up and the crew must figure out what to do. This episode is apparently based on the experience of a World War II Japanese soldier, Lieutenant Hiroo Onoda, and others, who during World War II had gone into hiding in the remote Philippine island of Lubang. When he was discovered in 1972, he thought the war was still going on.

Some of our defense mechanisms may function in this anachronistic way. The tyrannical self or bullying self often served an important protective function earlier in life, but now, though circumstances have changed, it nonetheless continues to think "the war is still on." For instance, a person may have evolved important defenses to aid in living with a critical, inappropriate, or abusive parent, but later, these old self-protective mechanisms are played out with other people in life who are not the same way, often with bad consequences.

The tyrannical self is that part of yourself that internalizes a critical, negative, and judgmental voice from someone, such as a parent, and "owns it" as the self. These harsh self-damning voices are woven into the very fabric of the self, and we may often use them to beat ourselves up for not being perfect. This may have been somewhat adaptive at an earlier point: by internalizing the criticism, for instance, there is at least a sense of control, and by shaming the self we may get a feeling of safety by not attracting too much attention to the self.

Mindfulness practice can help us see all these "ancient warriors"—our old defenses still fighting a war long over—to move attention out of the destructive and limiting stories and into the rich repository of feelings in the body.

Mindfulness helps to negotiate an end to the conflict.

58. Babysitting

Because you are an adult, you probably think your mind is adult too, and can function on its own without supervision. Of course we'd like to think our mind is mature, even sophisticated, but as often as not our mind may need some "babysitting" to keep it from getting into trouble.

A therapeutic intervention called Mindfulness-Based Cognitive Therapy (MBCT) helps to prevent relapse of future depressive episodes in patients who have had multiple episodes of depression. To accomplish this, participants use mindfulness to monitor their thoughts and feelings. They learn the connection between sad feelings and thoughts that are associated with depression. Because these distorted thoughts can catalyze episodes of depression, it is imperative to notice what is happening in the mind at all times. Sad feelings are a normal part of life and are experienced by everyone.

However, for someone who has experienced an episode of depression, these sad feelings can be the first step in a process that results in another episode of depression. When sadness arises, mindfulness is a babysitter. Mindfulness reminds the individual that sadness can be a normal feeling and that the thoughts arising in association with the sadness are just thoughts and not facts. Depression can be averted by feeling what is happening in the body in the moment and by not believing these thoughts or mistaking them for reality.

And you don't even need to pay mindfulness $15 an hour for the service!

59. "Move It or Lose It!"

When it comes to certain aspects of life, do you treat one day like any other? Do you feel bored or stuck in a rut?

Even though things seem the same, they are constantly changing—and even in mundane routine, we can learn to find richness and vividness of life as it unfolds. We tend to lump things into categories for efficiency, which is great when you are trying to avoid tigers on the savannah but not so well suited for the complex life we live today.

All the senses are tuned to novel experiences. When something is a constant perception, it gets "tuned out" of attention so that you can devote your resources to detecting new things. For the sake of adaptation and survival, new information is typically most important. This process is called habituation, and it is an important feature of sensation and perception.

Mindfulness can help you to appreciate the richness and variation that is present in the sameness of things. When you practice and pay close attention, you will notice that each breath feels a bit different. If you can appreciate the variation of the breath, the most pedestrian things in life can become sources of great satisfaction.

You don't have to go on exciting adventures to exotic places to feel alive. You can feel alive and engaged right where you are. In fact, mindfulness practice can be a permanent fix for boredom.

60. Two Arrows

The Buddha taught a metaphor of two arrows: The first arrow is the inevitabilities of life—pain, loss, illness, and the certainty of death. This arrow is unavoidable, and it will inevitably strike its target: every living being. The second arrow, however, is one we shoot at ourselves, creating a self-inflicted wound. And this wound is often greater than the first. It comes from the complicating storytelling activities of the mind, from all the ways the mind compounds anguish through its relationship to what is happening.

Check to see how much of your distress is the situation itself or your storytelling around this situation. When we create a self-inflicted wound with the second arrow, we are often in a state of denial; we are resisting reality, not accepting what is so. Or sometimes, we take the general misfortunes of life personally, making more misery out of the pain of being.

Pain is the first arrow; suffering is the second.

Mindfulness gives you the ability to sidestep the self-created "second arrows" of resistance and judgment, and at the same time bandage the inevitable wounds of impermanence.

61. "As Exciting as Watching Grass Grow"

I can see every morning that my lawn is getting longer. But if I sit and watch it nothing ever appears to be happening. Likewise, if we are constantly evaluating the global condition of our lives or our progress toward some important goal nothing much may seem to be happening. Yet if we can sit back and evaluate it less frequently or less intensively, we can appreciate our progress. This requires patience and forbearance. Change can be slow like the growth of grass.

Being impatient can be especially problematic when we are coping with a chronic or severe problem. If we can assume that with mindfulness practice, some kind of improvement in coping with this life-condition will occur over time, albeit slowly, then it would be a good strategy to spend less time continually asking yourself, "How is my life? Do I feel better right now than I did a moment ago, or less good? What about now?" Doing this less frees us up to focus on solving practical problems in the present and working toward achievable goals, and to attend to the things that are important. This helps to avert discouragement and despair that can arise when we insist that life should be transformed on the spot.

Mindfulness practice teaches us this patience and forbearance. When restlessness arises, we endeavor to stay in our seat and keep practicing. We bring ourselves back from the future and from global judgments about how things are going. Instead, the focus is on the present. Yet if we fast-forwarded all these present moments, like time-lapsed photography, we could appreciate the change that is unfolding right underneath our noses.

62. The Pause Button

Many electronic devices have a pause button—but, unfortunately, the mind does not seem to come equipped with one.

Just think how useful such a feature would be: when the mind starts spinning into angry reactivity, when our life throws devastating news our way, when anxious, fearful, overwhelmed feelings arise—what if we could just "press pause" before reacting? Good news: Mindfulness practice helps to supply just such a pause button. In fact, this is what mindfulness is: a pause.

All any of us need is a split second to interrupt the pattern of automatic reacting. In this tiny gap, we can recognize the possibility for choice. We can learn to be prompted to pause by cues from the body—the sense of warmth from increased blood flow that precedes boiling anger, feelings in the pit of the stomach, tension in the head, and so forth. Often we may have a characteristic way of registering feelings in the body and these feelings are often easier to recognize than patterns of thought, but certain patterns of thought can also be cues. However, the body will always provide a lot of information. If you can get that message you might have a chance to respond deliberately.

Just press pause.

63. Don't Fall Asleep at the Wheel

If you stray too far from your traffic lane on the Interstate, you will run over the "rumble strip"—those grooves in the pavement that make such a noise when you drive over them at high speeds, alerting you to the danger of driving off the road.

What can serve as your rumble strip for waking up from the stories of the mind? Without mindfulness, the only time we notice we've nodded off it is already too late: the damaging words have already been said, the ill-advised action already taken—we've already hit oncoming traffic. But with the practice of mindfulness, the body itself can serve as the rumble strip.

There is always something happening in the body before you react in words or behavior. There are warning signs waiting to be felt and responded to, if you can direct your attention to them. Under ideal circumstances, you would catch these feelings just as they start to develop. But in truth, it's helpful to notice them at any time. It is of course better to catch the reaction while it is still manageable, before it becomes a full-blown emotional reaction. And this requires practice.

So, the next time you feel the *BUMPABUMPA-BUMP* of your body's rumble strip, let it wake you up and call you right back to the present.

Metaphors for Acceptance, Resistance, and Space

Acceptance of reality as it is, is essential to the practice of mindfulness—and, of course, if we are not accepting, we are resisting. As the Buddha suggested, sometimes it can be helpful to think of acceptance and resistance in terms of "visitation": we can welcome our painful thoughts or difficult experiences to tea, as a good host does for any guest. At other times, it can be helpful to think of "creating space" around the experience that needs to be accepted. Such space can give us room to pause and to make better choices, to improve our relationship with the mind, and to "get perspective" on what is happening rather than simply getting sucked into its chaotic center.

"Resistance is futile," say the notorious cybernetic bad guys, the Borg, in the various *Star Trek* series. And, when it comes to the inevitable realities of life, the Borg are right. This is not to advocate passivity, acquiescence, or resignation. As cliché as it may have become, the wisdom of Rienhold Niebhur's "Serenity Prayer" holds true in asking for, "grace to accept with serenity the things that cannot be changed, courage to change the things that should be changed, and the wisdom to distinguish the one from the other."

Whatever progress you make in working through things, whether it is in psychotherapy or meditation practice, you will always continue to "receive visits" from bizarre and difficult thoughts, random images, harsh judgments, and unexpected emotions. And feelings and thoughts of resistance will inevitably continue to arise from time to time. The frequency and intensity of these thoughts may change over time, and this is one indication of "progress" in both therapy and mindfulness practice. But the fact that these thoughts still arrive for visits, however, should not be interpreted as a setback or a failure.

This is, after all, just the way the mind works.

64. Wild Chickens

Meditation teacher Larry Rosenberg tells a story of how after many years of studying as a Zen monk in Korea and Japan, he went to Thailand to study in the Thai forest tradition of Theravada Buddhism. He brought with him on this journey a set of expectations of what the experience would be like.

When he arrived, he was assigned to a small hut in the forest, with meals brought by an attendant at regular intervals. It was the ideal situation for furthering his meditation studies—except that the forest was also crawling with wild chickens whose primary occupation was running around squawking all day. Distressed and dismayed, he was confronted with his stories: "How can I meditate with all this noise?" he wondered, "This is ruining my experience!"

As it turns out, one of my neighbors is raising guinea hens. While not "wild chickens," they wander freely and make quite a racket, raising a cacophonous bellicose screech every time my hundred-pound Rhodesian ridgeback and I run by. I'm delighted: My very own wild chickens!

We always have a choice. If the reality of the situation contains wild noisy chickens, it can be resisted or accepted. We can be distressed and agitated or at peace.

Chances are that whenever you meditate, you'll have plenty of wild chickens to deal with. These include impatience, restlessness, boredom, and frustration. If you can set aside your ideas about how meditation (or your life as a whole!) *should be*, you will be moving closer to acceptance.

And who knows, maybe you'll come to equanimously appreciate the company of all those chickens!

65. The Buzzing Fly

Imagine a fly buzzing around you while you are engaged in meditation. Compassionately wanting not to harm it, you allow the fly to do what it does or gently whoosh it away with your hand. But the fly is annoying and keeps presenting itself to the tip of your nose or buzzing around your ears or landing on your cheek. What to do?

One option is to continue sitting and being annoyed, or to continue whooshing the fly away. Another is to expand the concept of your self in that moment to *include* your experience of the fly. After all, the reason the fly is annoying is because you've got some embedded rule or belief that says, "This fly should not be present; it is disturbing my meditation. My meditation should feel differently than it does now. It should be flyless." If that belief can be revised to include the fly, there is no longer opposition and no longer a problem. The revision eliminates the resistance.

Substitute disturbing, worrisome, or grotesque thoughts for the fly. The mere presence of such thoughts may be distressing. Distress follows from embedded rules, perhaps going something like: "A normal person doesn't have these thoughts. What is wrong with me? How horrible this is! I'm stuck. Doomed." The embedded rule/thought/expectation creates resistance and increases the sense of suffering that comes from this consternating piece of reality in the present moment.

If you can view these thoughts and reactions as the buzzing fly, you can make some deliberate choices about how you want to deal with their presence—including just patiently acknowledging and accepting them.

66. Weeds

You may prefer flowers to weeds. This may be a necessary approach to gardening, but can be vexing when dealing with thoughts. Some thoughts are like weeds; they are gangly, ugly, and proliferate wildly—and they can choke out other experiences we like better.

Shunryu Suzuki says of weeds, "You should be rather grateful for the weeds you have in your mind, because eventually they will enrich your practice." When it comes to the garden of the mind, it may be better not to put effort into pulling the weeds. Rather you can use the weeds to show you the places where you have disowned parts of your experience and yourself. In this way, they become a kind of fertilizer. What's more, you can even come to see that they have a kind of beauty just as they are, that in an important way each of the weeds is as perfect as the flowers.

Mindfulness practice will help you to become comfortable with the weeds and less invested in trying to get rid of them. And, after all, both weeds and flowers are products of the mind. Mindfulness cultivates the habit of observing thoughts as mental events without pressure to do anything special with them, without pressure to sort them into categories (weeds *bad*, flowers *good*). Just keep observing what comes up in the mind, weeds and flowers alike, and keep bringing your attention back to the present.

67. "If You Don't Like the Weather..."

In New England, people say if you don't like the weather, just wait for five minutes until it changes. This variability in weather is a good metaphor for the variability in moods. Some days are overcast and dark, others bright and sunny; to some degree, variation in mood is normal. Sometimes we're happy, other times we're sad.

And yet, just as we like to complain about the weather, we complain about our moods. But you can step back and observe them from the seat of mindfulness, they can pass by, just as the weather passes by. If we look closely, it's also the case that even a bad mood is constantly changing. Indeed, one of the fundamental insights of Buddhism is that all things are always changing.

If you try to treat things as if they don't change (or as if they can change by your command), suffering results. If you demand that the weather be a certain way—good luck! Sometimes you get lucky and the weather cooperates, but mostly it doesn't. If you need your mood, your ability to sleep, or anything else to be a certain way when it is not, you've got a recipe for suffering and dissatisfaction.

When you are stuck with something, be it inclement weather or inclement mood, can you accept it and redefine who you are in that moment to include whatever is going on? If you can, you are putting mindfulness into action—accepting reality without resignation.

68. "This Piece of Paper Is My Universe"

Take a pad of paper and hold it up to your face. This 8.5-by-11-inch sheet of paper looms so large in your visual field that it has become your universe in this moment; you can't see anything else at all. The pad itself has not changed, of course, but your perspective has.

Life events are like this pad. This is true whether we are talking about internal events like thoughts and feelings, or external ones like circumstances. In all cases, distress and suffering come from "getting too close" to these events and the thoughts and perceptions that accompany these events.

Mindfulness practice is akin to taking the pad of paper away from your face and holding it out at arm's length. Nothing has changed other than the relationship to that event. It's important to understand that this movement does not involve denial or resistance—you're not hiding the pad or fighting it off; the pad is still there and the writing on it still says whatever it says. Yet this action creates space, and what was previously consuming is now "in better perspective."

69. "I Am Ready to Accept Your Terms of Surrender"

The word "surrender" has many negative connotations—and yet, surrender can be a deep and rich form of acceptance.

Mindfulness meditation practice is a form of surrendering to what is happening now. It is surrendering to the moment without imposing an agenda or conditions on what must be so. When you pay attention to your body in the way that you do during meditation, you are practicing surrender. With surrender, resistance is diminished and acceptance is increased. Each small moment of surrender to the breath and to the body, such as noticing the way your breathing feels right now, can help to bring about acceptance or "deep surrender" to the more important events in life that may occur—especially those events you do not want, such as illness, loss, or setbacks.

In this way, we practice surrendering to the "small" moments in life to prepare for the "big" ones.

70. "Revolting!... Give Me Some More."

As Zen teacher Shunryu Suzuki writes, "In the beginner's mind there are many possibilities, but in the expert's there are few." The expert mind is beholden to concepts about the world, to judgments and categories, and can be rigid and inflexible. In certain cases, these concepts are quite arbitrary and limiting.

One splendid illustration of beginner's mind comes from the android Data in *Star Trek: The Next Generation*. Data is an emotionless being until he installs an emotion chip—and we get to observe his first emotional experience. In the movie, *Star Trek: Generations*, Data walks into the lounge of the ship and is promptly offered a drink.

> Guinan: "Gentleman, something new from Frocus 3?"
> *[Data drinks the substance, convulses and grimaces]*
> Giordi: "What?"
> Data: "I believe this beverage has produced an emotional response."
> Giordi: "Really!? What are you feeling?"

Data: "I am uncertain. Because I have so little experience with emotion, I am unable to articulate the sensation."

Guinan: "Emotion?"

Giordi: "I'll tell you later."

[Data drinks some more of the liquid]

Data: "Eeeuw!"

Guinan: "Looks like he hates it."

Data: *[smiling and staring at the glass]* "Yes, that is it! I hate this! Oooh yes, I hate this! It is… revolting!"

Guinan: "More?"

Data: "Please."

Data is experiencing his experience without judgment, and the result is openness to experience and the ability to welcome something "negative" without becoming distressed. He is showing that aversion does not have to be aversive.

Mindfulness practice helps to cultivate such a beginner's mind by treating every moment of life as unique. Mindfulness regards every moment with interest, curiosity, and awe.

71. To Give Your Sheep or Cow a Large Meadow Is the Way to Control Him

We have a tendency to want to get rid of what is difficult. We may want to banish unpleasantness from our consciousness, to rigidly fence off just the small part of the meadow of experience we like. When we do this, we find aspects of our life always jumping out of our fenced-off part and wreaking havoc. No matter how hard we try there are certain animals of the mind we can't control.

But as shepherds and farmers know, the best way to manage sheep is to give them a large meadow in which to graze. Here again we have a metaphor for acceptance. We don't have to fence the sheep in a tight pen or force the cow into a stall to control them—which is good news because doing so requires a lot of effort, energy, and monitoring. Instead, the animals are given the space to be, and we probably don't bump into them very often. We allow them to be and we direct our attention elsewhere.

Mindfulness practice helps us to create this large meadow. The large meadow is another way of thinking of big mind. By creating this meadow where everything arising in the moment can be held, we move toward acceptance.

72. Lean into the Sharp Points

The meditation teacher Pema Chödrön in her book *The Places That Scare You* talks about "leaning into" the sharp points of life. This seems counterintuitive—after all, wouldn't we want to stay away from the sharp points?

Moreover, when life throws the sharp points in your direction you have a choice. You certainly don't want to throw yourself on the sharp points with sufficient force to impale yourself. Start by leaning, taking on just as much as you can take on. With practice, you can take on more and more. By not avoiding so much of life, more life is lived.

Most mindfulness-based stress reduction courses don't start with relaxation techniques. Why? Wouldn't it make sense to help relieve people's stress and tension immediately? This would seem like a sensible way to approach things, but I don't introduce relaxation until the sixth week of the eight-week course. I find it's better to first learn the technique to deal with things as they are, rather than a technique that seems to be a way to "change" things. There are times when things cannot be changed and acceptance, rather than relaxation or change, is the only option. In this way, I encourage people to lean into the sharp points of their life while providing them with a tool that can help them do this.

73. The Sole of the Earth

There is an old story about a princess who ordered the world covered in leather so that she could walk the earth without soiling and hurting her feet. A wise counsel to her suggested that she cover her *feet* with leather instead—and thus shoes were invented.

Mindfulness practice is like the sole of the shoe. Mindfulness provides durable protection from the craggy and dangerous earth, yet does not expect the world to bow to the needs of the self.

The more you practice the tougher and thicker this sole becomes. The more mindfulness is incorporated into daily moments, the more protection you gain from life's vicissitudes.

74. The Swept Floor Never Stays Clean

If you sweep the patio in November after leaves have fallen, you wouldn't expect it to stay clear forever. The patio is like the mind. Mindfulness meditation practice can feel like sweeping the mind and clearing away all the thoughts strewn about making a big mess.

It's easy to get caught up in resentment toward these leaves: "Damn it, I just swept that floor!" Despite our protests, nature has another idea. The world doesn't care if we've swept the patio or how long it took us to do it. In the same way, the mind has its ways, and it doesn't really care about your agenda. The mind will continue to do what it does: give rise to thoughts. If you expect the mind to stay "swept," you are setting yourself up for disappointment.

Meditation will not "fix you"; it will not change things once and for all. Nothing can do this. Your job is to keep sweeping. Thoughts will continue to come and blow onto your clean-swept patio. Just sweep. No need to ask questions. No need to complain. Keep sweeping. You don't need to analyze, interpret, or fix the leaves; time after time, you just need to sweep, returning to this moment just as it is, again, again, again.

With continued practice, you can start to recognize the wisdom in not reacting, or if reactions arise (as they sometimes will) of not amplifying them and feeding them.

You can learn to enjoy the coming and going of the leaves—and even of the endless sweeping as well!

75. Petty Tyrants

We've already met the petty tyrant in the form of the tyrannical self, but in *Fire From Within*, Don Juan introduces another crucial aspect of the petty tyrant to Carlos Castaneda. A petty tyrant is "a tormentor... someone who either holds the power of life or death over warriors or simply annoys them to distraction." Petty tyrants are important because they help "warriors" to overcome self-importance.

Don Juan warns, "Self-importance is our greatest enemy" because we become weakened by feeling offended by the deeds and misdeeds of others. A petty tyrant, then, provides an important service in helping us to overcome self-importance.

There is a story about the spiritual teacher Gurdjieff that illustrates the metaphor of the petty tyrant. At Gurdjieff's ashram, a man whose job it was to serve tea did not have the sunniest disposition. He was crass, short with everyone, and generally unpleasant. The students complained about him constantly and rebuked him frequently. He was moonlighting as a petty tyrant. However, eventually he tired of the rebukes and left the ashram.

When Gurdjieff found out about this, he gave chase and persuaded the man to return. Why would Gurdjieff do this? Why would he deliberately set out to make things more unpleasant for his students? Such a petty tyrant is a gift. The servant, as a petty tyrant, was a great assistant teacher: every time he interacted with the students he was "pushing their buttons" of self-importance. Each time he provoked them into annoyance, frustration, or emotional reaction, he was providing a valuable service. He was showing the students the places they were stuck, attached to their reactions, always taking themselves too seriously.

You may find that you have an adversarial relationship to the petty tyrants in your life. You'd rather not have to deal with them. However, if you can change this relationship and welcome their arrival, this can help to transform the resistance. If you can say, "Thank you for showing me where my self-importance is; thank you for being a petty tyrant; now I can learn something important about myself," then you are on the road to liberation. This little coup is one of the great benefits of mindfulness practice. When you can bring gentle curiosity to whatever arises, you gain interest in what is happening. Jettison the angst and adversity. See it as an opportunity for learning and growth.

76. Falling Down

Recall the last time you saw a young toddler making her first steps. Recall the joy, the fascination, and the persistence she expressed as she sought to master walking. There is often delight in the falling and a boundless desire to get up and start all over again. This, almost literally, is an embodiment of the beginner's mind. So how can we bring this freshness to our adult versions of falling down—failing, making mistakes, being less than perfect?

There's an old Zen saying, "Fall down seven times, get up eight." Through mindfulness practice, we learn, when we fall, to pick ourselves up again without the extensive tirade, without deprivation mind making a drama out of it, without beating ourselves up for having fallen in the first place. Examine what happens the next time you stumble and fall—the next time you don't live up to your own or another's expectations. Can you be compassionate with yourself, as you would be if a person walking beside you fell to the ground? Can you pick yourself up off the ground, brush yourself off, and continue walking? Can you treat yourself as kindly as you would a toddler learning to walk?

This process of picking yourself up off the ground is what you do when you practice mindfulness. You fall down when you get engrossed in thoughts and stories and when you recognize this, you pick yourself up and begin again. This new beginning does not involve beating yourself up for having fallen down, for having gotten distracted.

See if you can embrace the enthusiasm of a young child. Fall and laugh. Get up with determination ready to fall again. Don't make falling a problem. Don't make getting up a production.

And, of course, don't assume you won't fall again.

77. Be the Mapmaker

Cartography is an apt metaphor for the attitude to take during meditation practice. A good mapmaker makes a careful study of the terrain and documents what is found. The mapmaker is neither for nor against any of the features that are found. The mapmaker does not say, "Well, I'd rather this river bend to the left instead of the right." This would not make a very useful map, after all. Yet, when you look at your own experience are you always trying to substitute one thing for another?

The instructions for mindfulness practice are to make a map of what you find with as much objectivity as possible. The aim is to bring a gentle curiosity to the practice and to greet whatever is found with even attention. This gentle curiosity directs attention to the moment-to-moment phenomena in the body at a descriptive level, so that you articulate what is present the way a cartographer would.

You can "map and observe" something as troublesome as pain, and thereby transform your negative experience of it. By exchanging the complaints of the storytelling mind for simple descriptions of physical features, you can make a useful map and start to feel less irritated. For instance, you might note: "Now there is tingling; now it's vibrating; now it's piercing; now it's sharp; now it's dull" and so on. Physical descriptions are neutral and do not evoke the same emotional reactions (and distorted, wishful maps) as the storytelling mind complaints.

With practice, you can start to notice that the body is comprised, in a way, of energy. The patterns of this energy are recognized by the brain, put into categories, and then given an emotional evaluation.

Why not sit down and draw yourself a good map of your experience right now?

78. Letting Go and Letting Be

Take a piece of paper and crumple it into a ball. Close your fist around it and turn your hand downward. Is this the state you are usually in?

It takes energy to hold that paper in your hand and there is resistance, contraction, and clenching. We often hear language that tells us to "let go" and to discard that piece of paper. Nevertheless, there are many situations that you cannot chuck, such as the death of a loved one or a chronic illness. So what can you do? You can try to throw the paper away, but it may be blown right back. But there's an alternative. Instead of chucking it, turn your hand over with your palm facing toward the sky and open your hand. This metaphoric action—what Zen teacher Kosho Uchiyama calls "opening the hand of thought"— creates space around the difficult situation, lowers the resistance, and changes how it affects you. This is letting it *be* versus letting it *go*.

Mindfulness will help you to let things remain as they are without always having to change them. This is not to say that practice will foster passive acquiescence. What it does say is that you can give up your preoccupation with things always having to be perfect. By letting things be, the mind can relax and enjoy what is present. You can look at an event or a feeling as if you were holding it in your open hand, palm facing up. You don't have to resist it, and you don't have to get rid of it. You can simply be with it.

79. "Tea. Earl Grey. Hot."

Can we make friends with all the parts of ourselves? This is the challenge presented by mindfulness practice. It's easy to welcome the parts of ourselves we like, but it is also easy to disown the difficult and challenging parts of the self. It seems counterintuitive to be nice to something that is dark, vexing, or harmful. "Befriending" is a form of acceptance, and acceptance is letting things be in this moment.

To accept is to befriend and to be a good host to your experience. Becoming a gracious host instead of a reluctant host is the promise offered by mindfulness.

You can welcome the visitation as part of your self, which in fact it is. Ram Dass talks of inviting neuroses for tea. In one talk, he describes one of his neuroses banging at the door. Instead of becoming disturbed or trying to push it away, he said, "Oh, sexual perversion, come in and have a cup of tea." Yet being a good host doesn't mean being an obsessive host. You don't have to cook your neurosis a ten-course meal. Just offer a simple cup of tea and tell it, "Enjoy your tea, while I continue doing whatever it was I was doing before you arrived."

Mindfulness practice with its even and curious attention does not express a preference for one type of experience over another. In this way, if we can be mindful of a pleasant sensation with the curiosity of the scientific mapmaker, then we can be mindful of an unpleasant sensation in the same way. We are befriending the entirety of experience. Equanimity can be thought of as befriending all experience with a calm, matter of fact, and abiding attention.

80. "Bring Me a Mustard Seed"

At an intellectual level we all know we are going to die. Yet can we really feel this truth openly, know it in our hearts and bones? Or do we subtly or not-so-subtly live in denial about this ultimate inevitability?

The Buddha was known as "The Great Physician" and renowned for his healing powers. One day, a young woman, Kisa Gotami, came to him with her newly dead child. She approached him and pleaded with him to restore the life of her precious son. She felt she could not go on without him. Out of compassion, the Buddha agreed to help the young mother. He said to her, "I will do as you ask, but first you must bring me a mustard seed from a home that has never known death." Grateful, she eagerly set out going home to home, village to village, in search of this mustard seed.

Of course, she returned empty-handed. But she gained something else: her journey gave her insight into a fundamental truth—everyone has tasted death. From this place of understanding, Kisa Gotami became one of the Buddha's disciples.

It can be helpful for all of us to remember that we do not suffer alone. This too is one of the gifts of mindfulness.

81. Pain and Suffering

Pain is not synonymous with suffering. Meditation teacher Shinzen Young offers the following formula:

suffering = pain x resistance

Pain is the label the brain applies to certain patterns of sensations present in the body. This pattern of sensation will have a negative emotional flavoring because negative affect can be an important motivation to action (such as moving your hand off of a hot burner, for instance). However, this feeling, while unpleasant, is not the same as suffering.

Suffering arises out of what you may tell yourself about the pain. In fact, when "the pain" becomes "my pain," suffering arises. "My pain" has a history and a future. "My pain" is embedded in a story of loss, frustration, and the anticipation of future suffering.

Mindfulness comes down to greeting your experience with openness and curiosity and reining in your tendency to add to any situation with the storytelling mind. Take for example, what Tiger Woods said, commenting on his knee surgery, just after taking the third round lead of the 2008 U.S. Open: "If pain hits, pain hits. So be it. It's just pain."

Likewise, as I am writing this, I have pain in my shoulder. It feels heavy, dull, and piercing as if a shovel had been inserted into my neck and shoulder blade and broken off, leaving the jagged metal behind. The next day it is worse, the jagged metal has become even sharper, more acute, and the surrounding muscles stiffen around it. I am confronted by choices almost every moment that my attention is drawn to this pain. I can choose to make it into a problem or I can accept it and receive it as part of my experience.

In this acceptance, I aim to take care of myself by modifying my activities while not becoming overprotective. I can be aware simultaneously that the pain is present and unpleasant, and then just leave it at that. It does not have to diminish my sense of well-being in the moment, I do not have to medicate it into submission, and I don't have to revise the story of myself to accommodate it. In a basic way, it just is, and if I can resist the temptation to defy reality and insist things should be other than they actually are, I'll be okay. While I have pain, I don't have suffering because I am not resisting. By not panicking and overprotecting, and by taking appropriate care of it, it feels better the next day, smaller and less intense. I resume my normal activities. This is acceptance in action.

82. "Why Didn't I Kneel More Deeply to Accept You?"

The poem "Tenth Duino Elegy" by Rainer Maria Rilke provides a metaphor for resistance and acceptance in a most problematic area: negative feelings. In that poem, Rilke actually sings praise to the tears on his face and the process of his weeping. He doesn't lament the negative feelings. He asks, "Why didn't I kneel more deeply to accept you?" He cautions that we "squander our hours of pain."

Our culture often conveys the message that any negative feelings are abnormal and can and should be "treated" in every case (and this is of course good business for Big Pharm). But through mindfulness practice, we can start to befriend the arising of negative feelings, and come to see they are normal—or even useful as Rilke suggests in his poem. Taken to an extreme, advertising for anti-depressant medications conflates normal variations in human mood for treatable medical conditions. One is not necessarily the other, although one is always part of the other.

What if anxiety and other negative feelings could teach you something? Could you befriend them then?

While I am not suggesting that you celebrate negative feelings, I am suggesting that you increase your curiosity for them. Don't resist them automatically. Experiencing normal levels of anxiety and sadness does not diminish you or truly harm you in any way. Mindfulness practice can help you to know what is "normal" and what exceeds normal (sometimes anxiety and depression can become so extreme as to be incapacitating, and in such cases it is a wise choice to intervene medically even as you practice acceptance).

Acceptance of what is present in your experience can often help to make a shift. By making room for anxiety, it may subside because you are no longer feeding it with the storytelling mind of resistance.

Can you make friends with all of your feelings?

83. A Foot in the Door

One day, soon after I moved into my home, there was a knock at the door. An older man presented himself as an Electrolux salesperson and wanted to sell me a vacuum. Since the house had a central vacuum system, I thanked him for his offer and refused simply. But the visit started me thinking metaphorically about how certain things come to visit the mind "trying to sell" the self something—anger, fear, a low self-image, for instance.

There are many strategies for dealing with salespeople trying to sell you something that you don't need. They want to get a "foot in the door." It is unlikely that you interrupt the seller in the midst of his pitch to say, "Just tell me how much to make the check for!" Yet, this is the way we may "buy" our own thoughts wholesale.

Even with our own minds, we can listen to the sales pitch and politely say, "No, thanks," and let that be that. Sometimes, just as with salespeople, we may have to say, "No, thanks," a couple of times. But it's often so hard to do this, isn't it? How often are we getting a mental "sales pitch" and instantly reaching into our pockets for the checkbook? And even on the infrequent occasion we can muster the wherewithal to say "No, thanks" once, how often do we feel a kind of guilt for not buying the mind's story, even when we don't want what is being sold?

One strategy we can apply to "door-to-door" salespeople in our own minds is to "look out the peephole" to see who is at the door. If it is a salesperson—the familiar stories and judgments of our mind—mindfulness gives us a space to choose not to open the door.

We don't have to buy everything the mind tries to sell us just because the salesperson is between our ears.

Mindfulness will help you to become less beholden to your thoughts, less of an "easy mark" to the inner salespeople.

84. Office Hours

University professors post office hours. Mine were once Tuesdays 3:15 to 4:15 p.m. and Fridays 1:00 to 2:00 p.m. Students knew I was available during those hours. If they couldn't make one of these times, they must make an appointment. Faculty do not make themselves available all of the time; often the door is closed so that other work may get done.

When it comes to your mind, however, do you give thoughts 24/7 access? Do you worry all throughout the day and even in the middle of the night? Are you constantly on call to your mind?

A benefit of mindfulness practice is developing cognitive boundaries akin to office hours. We don't have to give noisome thoughts unlimited free access to attention and consciousness.

One tool that I teach people is *scheduled worrying*. Like office hours, a dedicated time is given to worry and kvetching. During this time you mindfully allow yourself to project into the future, mull over the past, write things down, problem-solve, and dwell on fears and worry about outcomes. And then, when thoughts present themselves with urgency outside of this dedicated time, you can remind them with gentle firmness that office hours are at 3 p.m. and they'll be dealt with then.

Mindfulness practice develops the skills required to set up "inner office hours."

85. Monkey Trap

In India, an ingenious trap is used to catch monkeys. It is a simple box with bars spaced wide enough for a flat hand to go through. In the box is placed a tasty banana. A monkey can reach into the box through the bars to grasp the banana. However, the monkey cannot extricate its hand while clutching the prized fruit—its fist is too big for the bars. If the monkey holds on, it will stay caught. If it can let go and abandon the banana, it can possibly get out of the box. With our thoughts, of course, we are just like this monkey, clinging to all kinds of things at our peril.

This is reminiscent of destructive patterns of thinking. The more you think, the more distressed you become. Why? Because you cannot think yourself out of a problem that thinking got you into in the first place. Rumination rarely helps to solve a problem. Additional thinking cannot alleviate the distress that rumination creates. The point of diminishing returns has long since passed.

Another trap image comes from the "Chinese finger trap" puzzle. This clever and simple device is a tube of woven straw. In each end, you stick a finger. If you try to pull your fingers out of the puzzle, the woven material clamps down on your fingertips. The more you pull the more it clamps. The more you resist the more it has you. The only way out of the finger trap is to go more deeply in, to actually push your fingers toward each other and toward the grasping trap—then it expands and loosens. This is, of course, an excellent metaphor for the ineffectuality of resisting our experience and the utility of "leaning in" to unwanted experience.

Mindfulness practice provides a solution to resistance. Whenever we can recognize that we are caught in the monkey trap or the Chinese finger puzzle, mindfulness gives us the opportunity to extricate ourselves. To free ourselves from the monkey trap, we just need to let go of clinging. To free ourselves from the finger trap, we need to "lean into" difficulty rather then reacting from aversion and resistance.

86. Mental Aikido

Aikido is a martial art that promotes peace and non-violence over war. Aikido utilizes graceful circular movements to neutralize an attack: it uses the energy that is already present and takes it in the direction that it is going, letting an assailant's own momentum fling him harmlessly away. The aims of Aikido moves are to be "true" (effective at accomplishing its goal of averting an attack), "good" (not harming the assailant or oneself), and "beautiful to behold."

Mindfulness is a kind of "mental Aikido." Mindfulness is not blind force against force (combating the assailing thoughts) and mindfulness is not avoidance (turning tail and fleeing difficult circumstances). As with Aikido, you make contact with what comes at you, whatever it is. Contact is not resisted nor is it pursued—and it doesn't involve struggle.

In plain and profound terms, you deal with what is real in the moment.

87. The Cluttered Garage

Imagine a cluttered garage. You can't walk two steps without bumping into some old junk and stubbing your toe. It's the same way in the mind; you can't walk two steps without bumping into some painful memories, rigid self-perception, or unyielding belief about yourself and the world. Our minds are full of these things, and meditation is not going to eradicate these thoughts. Instead, mindfulness practice helps to create the sense of spaciousness without creating more junk. Mindfulness is a way of enlarging the cluttered garage of our minds. And occasionally, you might even get an opportunity to throw out a piece of useless junk.

There is another similar metaphor about salt in water. A tablespoon of salt in a cup of water will be intensely salty—but the same tablespoon in a gallon will be barely perceptible. The more space that can be put around the things that bother you, the less bothersome they are. Mindfulness practice helps to create such space.

88. "The Best Seats Are in the Balcony"

Have you noticed that when you get too close to your difficult experiences, you tend to suffer more? The drama may be too intense, and it is hard to breathe in that confined space. It can be helpful to imagine sitting in the audience watching the play rather than being in the middle of the drama on the stage. Yet, the play itself can be so compelling, can't it?

First, you must notice that there is a moment of choice, that you can step back and there is a space in which to do that—the large empty theater surrounding the stage. Second, you must be willing to create the vantage point to the center of the drama. This may require giving up something that you are holding on to, such as being right, or getting recognition. With practice, it can even be fun to step back and to watch yourself and those around you with this bit of detachment. Instead of becoming overwhelmed by someone's anger or words, you can try to appreciate their struggle.

During the final evening of my eight-week class, a loud noise arose during meditation. Someone was cleaning in the foyer just outside the studio, and he was having a difficult time. Not realizing that people were meditating just beyond the door and within earshot, the cleaner struggled with a mop and bucket and there was a loud crashing noise and many expletives. From the space of meditating, the absurdity of his behavior was evident. So too was the suffering that he was generating for himself. The participants in the class directed some compassion in his direction. When you can step from the stage and sit in the audience—maybe in a nice box seat up in the balcony—you can appreciate the often absurd and painful nature of your own behavior. Sitting in the audience, you can choose your response instead of reacting impulsively.

Mindfulness practice makes our meditation seat into a balcony seat—the best seat in the house!

89. Sky Mind

Thoughts pass through the mind like clouds in the sky. Sometimes during meditation, it is as if you are in a thunderstorm with thick heavy clouds; sometimes the internal weather is only a few wispy clouds; and sometimes there are no clouds at all, just big blue sky. What is called original mind or big mind is what lies beyond the clouds. Your mind is not just the thoughts; it is not just the passing clouds. The mind is also the whole sky itself, with or without clouds.

Mindfulness practice is a process for watching the clouds, noticing them, without trying to change them or to get rid of them. When you watch the clouds without any storytelling mental activity, they may tend to dissipate—opening to a clear sky. But it's important to also recognize that the sky is still vast and open, even on overcast days.

90. "Don't Waltz in the Minefield"

Life can really catch you off guard sometimes, can't it?

John Philpot Curran, an eighteenth-century Irishman and member of the parliament, said that "Eternal vigilance is the price of liberty." We might also say that continual mindfulness is the price of freedom from self-created suffering.

Sometimes life can be like a minefield, and so we must be vigilant, cautious, and awake. If we run carelessly across the field, we will likely suffer great harm. When we are aware we are entering a minefield it's easy to remember to be careful, to be mindful. But what about all the myriad circumstances when the danger is not quite so cut and dry? Mindful vigilance, to our own reactivity and our stories, is important even then.

The aim, of course, is not to be obsessive about every potential situation, paralyzed by a lot of fearful restriction, but rather to acknowledge the reality that it may occur and to honor that reality with a measure of caution.

Mindfulness practice helps you to be prepared for the unexpected. In the process of becoming intimate with the feeling body, you have a head start on tracking emotional reactions. This head start can help you to prevent acting upon these emotional reactions or to recover quickly once a reaction begins.

In this way, you can cultivate *mine-field-ness*!

Metaphors for Practice

For some people, beginning meditation practice is like returning home. For many, though, meditation can be unfamiliar and difficult—and hard to sustain. Metaphors for practice can be helpful in making practice more accessible and effective.

The metaphors in this section will help you to make a space in your life for meditation. These metaphors will help you to persist when your gumption is flagging and the other demands in your life are pressing. But the bottom line is clear: if you want to get some value out of mindfulness, you must actually practice being mindful. And, like the development of any skill, this requires effort. But this effort does not need to be arduous—practice also lets you connect to a more joyful, natural, and ease-filled form of effort. It can be like floating on a raft in a gentle surf, riding the waves of the in-breath and the out-breath.

91. "Please Take Your Seat"

When we speak of "taking your seat" for meditation, we often imagine sitting down in the lotus position— but more broadly, the true meditation seat is any posture used mindfully, and so it also includes sitting, walking, standing, and lying down. More broadly still, the seat is also the attitude you bring to practice. The body can sit down, and the mind must sit down too. I always invite my students during a guided meditation to take *both* of these seats: the posture and the attitude for practice.

With continued practice, the seat will become a stable base from which to practice. It will hold you when you are restless, agitated, and impatient and it will keep your butt on the cushion. The seat can be a wonderful place. It can be helpful to honor and support the seat by designating an area of your home just for meditation. Having this special place won't do the meditation for you, but it can promote practice.

92. The Stillness Between Two Waves of the Sea

The ocean knows a thing or two about patience.

The ocean will spend eons breaking big rocks into sand. It makes the same tidal movements every day without complaint. It touches land with surf, wave upon wave. The rhythmic rolling of the surf is like breathing. It is inexorable and elemental.

Can you be patient like the surf? Can you follow the tide of the breath as it moves through the day?

T.S. Eliot in the *Four Quartets* recognizes the power of the sea when he says: "But heard, half-heard, in the stillness / Between two waves of the sea."

As you attend to waves of breathing, also experiment with focusing farther "offshore," not on the surf crashing into the beach, but on the great rising and falling swells in the distance. This too, the moment when one wave swells and subsides, is a metaphor for breathing; in the tiny gap between the in-breath and the out-breath you can find that stillness that T.S. Eliot writes about. In certain meditation traditions, this gap is itself a focus of practice, that moment between breaths when the exhalation has finished but the inhalation has not yet begun.

In mindfulness practice, sometimes it can be helpful to picture the breath as the moving sea as you sit watching and feeling the breath. In doing so, you can come to recognize a continuity between your breathing self and the breathing of nature.

93. Holding a Baby Bird

A baby bird is a dynamic and fragile creature. Hold it too loosely and it will fly away. Hold it too tightly and it may get crushed. This image can be helpful for how you apply effort in meditation practice. Too little effort and the mind will escape and fly away like the bird. Too much effort and you may crush your spirit. The right approach is not too tight and not too loose.

Effort is a tricky topic, especially in the achievement- and goal-oriented cultures of the West. This always reminds me of a cartoon in *The New Yorker* that shows a man entering an elevator. In response to the elevator operator's standard query ("Going up or down?"), the man says, "Neither up nor down, I'm good here." We are so conditioned to always be *doing something* that simply *being* seems alien or even downright un-American!

And so it is with meditation. The ego will take over anything that involves achievement and goals. How often have we had some version of the thought that, "If I am now going to become a meditator then by gosh I'll become an *excellent* meditator!" And then what happens when we don't live up to our ego-centered demands? We feel like a failure, of course.

The ego's energy can be helpful at first but soon becomes a limiting trap. With mindfulness practice, it is not the minutes of meditation racked up on the cushion or the miles traveled to distant retreats or time spent with renowned teachers. It just is the process of becoming intimate with the mind, of not reacting, and being free.

The ego wraps itself around the practice and can become bossy. It can make meditation into something arduous, and the striving (itself a form of doing) gets in the way of simply being, which is the ultimate goal of the practice. Of course, we want to have goals and to put effort toward achieving them. We wouldn't get far without them.

Have goals, but don't be attached to them. Hold the bird, care for it, but don't crush it.

94. Sharpening the Axe

If you have a huge pile of wood to cut and a limited amount of time to do it in, you may conclude you have no time to stop and sharpen your axe, and so you just keep hacking away with an increasing dull blade in a frantic attempt to get the job done. But it makes more sense, though, to stop and spend the necessary time to sharpen the axe.

Mindfulness meditation practice sharpens the axe of the mind. Taking five or ten minutes out of a busy work hour to be mindful can actually make you more productive. Taking an hour out of the day that is already overbooked can help you to live in a more balanced and energized way. Making the time to practice is key, and whatever time is invested in practice will pay its own dividends of increased clarity, energy, focus, and contentment.

95. The Reality on 7th Avenue

Meditation may conjure images of the exotic—remote Himalayan caves, colorful Buddhist monks, golden buddhas, and dancing images of Shiva. But mindfulness meditation is nothing special; in fact, it's rather ordinary.

The playwright Wallace Shawn captured this sense of the ordinary in the film *My Dinner With Andre* when he said:

> Why do we require a trip to Mount Everest in order to perceive one moment of reality? Is Mount Everest more real than New York? Isn't New York real? I think, if you could become fully aware of what existed in the cigar store next to this restaurant, I think it would just blow your brains out! Isn't there just as much reality to be perceived in the cigar store as there is on Mount Everest?

Nature and reality are around us at all times; the mind has a tendency to overlook the sacredness of the mundane. Each moment affords some beauty, some element of peace, and some opportunity for connection.

Mindfulness practice will familiarize you with the extraordinary ordinary. Each moment that you are mindful is a mini-awakening. Even a trip down 7th Avenue can be exhilarating, like scaling Everest.

96. The Sitar of Enlightenment

A sitar string that is too slack will give no sound. A string that is too tight may snap. Likewise, when you practice, your approach should be neither too slack nor too tight.

The idea is not to be obsessive about and bound by rules (tightening the string too much) while also not being completely willy-nilly or undisciplined (loosening the string). If we become too identified with the rules (even the "rules" of mindfulness practice) then we are caught in attachment. And yet when we are lacking in discipline, the mind is slack and cannot produce a clear sound. And of course, without the discipline of mindfulness, we may create so much noise in our life that we cannot hear the instrument of the mind playing. So, the middle way is to approach practice with a firm yet gentle hand.

97. Learning to Play a Musical Instrument

You wouldn't expect to pick up a trombone for the first time and be able to play it. After all, learning a musical instrument requires practice. Likewise, learning meditation takes time and practice. Developing the habit of mindfulness requires concentrated work and effort.

It is said that it takes 10,000 hours of doing something to become an expert in it. That's the equivalent of five years of fulltime work, or one hour a day for thirty years. The good news, however, is that you don't have to be an expert in meditation to derive benefit from mindfulness or to incorporate it into daily life. As few as eight weeks of regular practice might show demonstrable changes in your life and even in your brain itself. It may take some adjustment in attitude to see attention as a skill that is subject to development and refinement. Nevertheless, like learning any skill, practice is essential.

Play the instrument of your mind often!

98. "Just Do It!"

Although attention is a process and not a muscle, it can be helpful to think of attention through a fitness metaphor. Attention improves with practice, growing more toned and responsive.

In weight training, there are periods of plateau where the creation of muscle mass levels off. This can happen in meditation too. You may hit plateaus, rough patches, and difficulties. The path in meditation may not be a linear one, reaching up with inexorable progress.

The trick is to realize that meditation is not about achievement—there is no mindful equivalent of being able to benchpress more and more weight. It is not about reaching a destination. It is about getting to know yourself. Who knows what you might find?

Some people find having a personal trainer helpful for establishing and maintaining an exercise program, and, similarly, a meditation teacher can also be helpful. Using guided meditations also provides structure and support—a kind of workout routine for the mind.

99. Divide and Conquer

The meditation teacher Shinzen Young in *Break Through Pain* talks about "dividing and conquering." You can't swallow the entire future or the entire past. You can't deal with an illness or pain for the "rest of your life"—yet you *can* deal with it in *this* moment, and then in the next moment, and so on. By "dividing" a seemingly monolithic task or daunting problem into its constituent moments, we can "conquer" one step and moment at a time. What's more, when we do this, we start to see how much of the difficulty we encounter has to do with the *idea* of the task or problem, rather than the real moments of the thing itself.

I encountered an excellent example of this in my own life this past winter. In Northern New England, where I live, it snows—a lot. During one storm, it snowed two feet. My driveway is over one hundred feet long. That is a lot of snow—thinking about it, it must be literally *tons* of snow. Pondering the sheer weight of all that snow together, I didn't think I could possibly do it.

But instead of thinking of the whole thing, I made an effort to just mindfully move one shovelful. And then another. And one more. Eventually, I cleared a path, one shovel-full at a time, over the course of a very long time.

I made it a form of meditation practice, being in the moment and attending to the embodied feelings of exertion and cold. The action was repetitive and rhythmic like the breath. If I looked down to the end of the driveway, I complained, "Oh my god, I'll never get this done." "Keep shoveling," I encouraged myself. All the familiar objections arose—impatience, wanting to be somewhere else—and these flowed into peaceful movement, one shovelful of snow at a time. Eventually, the job got done despite the doggy mind's complaints. Moreover, most of the task was enjoyable, and offered the feeling of accomplishment when finished.

To see another example of how something huge can be accomplished small part by small part, consider a huge bale of feathers. This massive amount would, taken together, weigh a ton. Yet, each feather is almost imperceptibly light. Practicing mindfulness is the practice of gently and patiently moving one light feather after another—this is the action of bringing the mind back in the moment.

When you can approach large tasks—or even small ones—as you would approach formal meditation practice, you can get a lot done. The practice of mindfulness meditation trains us in steady persistent effort.

This effort keeps returning to the task-at-hand with equanimity, forgiveness, and moments of laughing at yourself.

100. Be Prepared

You don't need to be a Boy Scout to appreciate the value of preparation. There is some preparation we'd never think of leaving to the last moment: we'd never consider going on a days-long hike up a huge mountain without buying and packing all the proper gear and food, and hardly anyone one would bear out a full term of pregnancy without making some plans for the baby.

Similarly, you'd be well advised to practice mindful meditation in the good times so that you have something to draw on when you need it, the times when things get tough. And things will get tough for everyone, eventually—minimally we will all inevitably encounter sickness, old age, death, loss, change in ourselves and those around us whom we love. So what form can this preparation take?

Here I'd like to introduce two terms: *formal* and *informal* practice. Formal practice is the time you spend on the cushion, walking, or doing mindful yoga practice, for instance. Formal practice occurs when you are doing *nothing but* mindfulness meditation. Informal practice, on the other hand, is when your formal practice "spills over" into everyday life: you are mindful while washing the dishes, taking out the garbage, working in the garden, talking to your kids, and all of the other activities of life.

For almost everyone, it takes formal practice to tap into and enjoy the benefits of informal practice. It can be easy to get caught up in formal practice and to be impressed with yourself for how many minutes and hours you are meditating and how wonderful are the rarefied mental states you may touch. But if this does not result in more time being mindful off the cushion, it's not very useful at all.

The goal of mindfulness is not to be mindful some of the time, but to be mindful *all* of the time—to really live every moment of your life. Formal practice is best viewed not as an end in itself but as a means to the end of mindful living.

101. "Come Back Soon!"

The goal of mindfulness meditation practice is to learn how to "come back" to this moment—yet many people mistakenly see the goal as sitting still with a quiet mind.

The primary problem is that people get the idea in their head that there is a "right" way to practice, and frustration arises if they are not "getting" it. Many people believe they "can't meditate" because they are not in the "right" frame of mind or because their mind is "too busy."

What they really mean to say is that when they did sit down to meditate, they found their mind filled with distraction, impatience, or boredom; or they were dealing with painful material that was presenting itself.

You may want meditation to be pleasant and meditation often is, but not necessarily. What's more, once you have a peaceful and relaxing meditation experience, the mind registers this as the benchmark for meditation and seeks to recreate it in each meditation. It compares all future meditation to this pleasant or powerful experience and is often disappointed that it is not the same. This is one of the major pitfalls on the path of learning mindfulness meditation, and it can be dangerous and seductive even for experienced practitioners.

When I teach mindfulness I emphasize the "coming back." So even when—or *especially* when—the mind is agitated, there is a practice we can always do: we can always practice coming back. The more agitated our mind, the more opportunities we have to practice coming back.

The goal of mindfulness practice is to work with what is, whatever that is in the moment. This simple instruction gets sidetracked all the time by expectations such as "meditation should be relaxing," "meditation should be peaceful," or "I'm so distracted, there is no point in meditating." These beliefs are common obstacles to practice. When you can focus on "coming back" rather than "staying put," you can never do it wrong—as long as you are coming back. Let me repeat that: *There is no way to do it wrong!* It doesn't matter if you were gone in the storytelling mind for one minute, ten minutes, or an hour, coming back *is* the practice. As it turns out, it is when the mind is agitated that is actually the most valuable time to practice because this is the mind that you must often deal with. Being inundated by thoughts is much more common than being in a settled place, so work with whatever your mind gives you with attention—even when the mind is in turmoil.

Practice coming back, with a matter-of-fact patience, to this moment just as it is.

Repeat as necessary.

102. "Sit... Sit... Sit... Good Puppy!"

Imagine a puppy, just eight or ten weeks old, that you are trying to train to sit. You tell it, "Sit." Perhaps it sits for a moment, and then it is off to play, to pee on the rug, shred newspaper, and generally to do what puppies do. You bring it back and try again, "Sit." Chances are you do this with a smile and a great deal of patience. Likely, most people would find it easier to be patient with the dog than with themselves in a new or difficult situation. I bet you rarely treat yourself as well as you would treat an animal! Or, to put it the other way, you would never treat a dog the way you treat yourself.

Why is this? How often do we treat ourselves with some degree of harshness? We beat ourselves up for the smallest things—the wrong word uttered, some minor imperfection? What if we could be gentle, loving, and forgiving with ourselves, as we would be with an adorable puppy?

Mindfulness practice helps you to develop this capacity. The instructions are clear on this issue. When attention wanders like the puppy, bring it back with gentleness. Don't scold yourself for the mind having wandered. It's just what minds do. Start again with the next breath. Repeat with a smile.

103. Hold On for Dear Life

When things get tough in life, it can seem like you are riding a bull in a rodeo. Especially when life is bucking hard, the temptation is to let go and get flung to the ground. The bulls in your life may be financial pressures, deadlines at work, aging parents, or a difficult child. Life keeps kicking. It's easy to fall off the bull by engaging in behaviors that comfort yet are not good for you. You may find yourself reaching for food or alcohol or zoning out in front of the television. It is counterintuitive to move toward what is challenging you and to hold on to the bull. If you fall off, the challenge is to get back on and keep riding. This can describe life in general or an individual session of meditation.

Mindfulness practice can help you to develop this bull-riding skill. As you sit and watch the breath, the meditation seat is like a saddle, both the seat on the ground and the seat in your mind. Hold on to each moment; practice not letting yourself be bucked off by the vigorous jumping and shaking of your mind. If you practice this, hour after hour of watching and feeling the vicissitudes of the mind will prepare you for handling the bull in everyday life. The key is to stay on the cushion when things get tough.

That bull will show up during meditation itself. The bull can start kicking during meditation, throwing all manner of tempting, bizarre, or intense feelings, thoughts, or images your way. You may think there is no point in meditating with such a racket going on. But keep it up anyway.

If you can ride the bull during this mindfulness meditation session, you can face down any challenge!

104. March of the Penguins

A silent meditation retreat is the traditional way to learn mindfulness. Typically, such a retreat is in a quiet country environment, or at least in a protected environment within a city. This protection allows the participants the opportunity to go deep within themselves to learn this method of meditation, and this can be valuable. However, it is not the only way to learn meditation.

Popular images of meditation include the remote cave on the mountaintop. There is a sense that to learn to meditate is to somehow remove oneself from the world—even the word *retreat* itself can conjure such an image.

My meditation studio in Burlington, Vermont, is located in a storefront on a busy street. There was noise from cars, buses, and people walking by. This might seem like a disadvantage for learning to meditate. However, it only remains a disadvantage if we cling to the secluded and quiet image of meditation practice. If we learn to meditate in this bustling environment, and everyone does, then we have something to take with us out in the world.

The popular film *March of the Penguins* portrays the precarious journey of penguins giving birth to the next generation. The severe cold of the Antarctic tundra makes the process perilous. The fledging chicks need protection from the temperatures that fall to -80° F. We must learn to care for our mindfulness practice as the new penguin parents care for the egg and the fledging young.

Learning to meditate and practice mindfulness does not need to be an epic expedition. However, it can be helpful to protect your fledgling practice by having a specific place in your home to practice. It can also be helpful to protect your practice by setting aside a special time each day to practice. Such protections can help to facilitate learning and help you to incorporate mindfulness into every aspect of life.

105. The Clothes Don't Make the Man

Mindfulness is an adaptable philosophy and psychology. It is a practical tool for coping with stress, pain, anxiety, and depression. It is a way to enhance life by making it more vivid. It can also be a tool for "salvation" from suffering.

And so it is easy to become enchanted with being a meditator. You can buy the cushions, the bells, the incense, and very much look and act like a person who meditates. You can even come to believe you are a great meditator and make it a part of your identity. Thoreau knew of this pitfall in 1854 when he said, "Beware of all enterprises that require new clothes, and not rather a new wearer of clothes." When the ego takes over the enterprise of mindfulness, it is a pitfall of practice.

It is good to have goals and to motivate yourself to practice. To be sure, practice requires effort. However, if we start to *identify* with the goals and the effort, or come to regard them as ends in themselves, we're in trouble. After all, this identification with being "a meditator" or to clothes—all the trappings and rituals of meditation—is just another story we are telling ourselves, and as such, it is just another mental formation we "come back from" into the here and now.

So, practice with effort, interest, and joy. Be with the process itself and don't get hung up on the trappings of enlightenment.

106. AAA for the Mind

It wouldn't make sense to live your life by dreading adversity but never preparing for it. Consider, for example, the spare tire in your car. You don't want a flat tire, of course, but you recognize the possibility and take precautions. Better still, you might subscribe to AAA.

Mindfulness practice cannot prevent every flat tire, but it does provide the means for handling that flat. It is the spare tire, the jack, and the expertise to make the change. Mindfulness can also provide maps and travel guidance as does AAA. Practice familiarizes us with the territory of the mind and can help us to navigate difficult "driving conditions" when they arise. Mindfulness can help us to be more self-sufficient handling difficult emotions and situations. Practicing on a regular basis helps to keep the "subscription" current.

You don't want to find your AAA card expired when you are stranded by the side of the road.

107. Squeeze the Sponge

Madison Avenue and many self-help books seem to hold out the possibility of instant transformation, one moment (or, more often, one *product*) and instantly and forever all our problems are solved. But real change is a slow, iterative process.

One day I was washing my car with a big natural sponge. While cleaning up, I dunked the sponge and it seemed to be free of soap but when I squeezed it, soap emerged. I dunked once more; again it appeared clear but upon squeezing it, more soap. This is what change is like. We are like the soapy sponge, comprised of thirsty cells that hold on to things like ideas, memories, and beliefs. When you feel good, it seems like the sponge of the mind is clear, but with the slightest perturbation, the soapy residue emerges.

Each time you meditate, it is like taking the sponge and dunking it in cool, clean water. You can feel clearer and lighter in your being after meditation. Sometimes, you can feel the exiting debris, the unwanted thoughts, memories, images, and emotions. Whatever comes up and out during practice helps you to become clear. But, I'm sorry to say, unlike the sponge that eventually can be made completely free of soap with enough dunking and squeezing, we won't ever become completely clear of mental junk.

And yet, with continued mindfulness practice, we can come to appreciate the journey, the process, rather than the destination or goal. After all, you can never take one breath and have that be enough for the rest of your life. You can never have one meal, no matter how large or delicious, and never have to eat again. You can never get one good night of sleep to last a lifetime. Each moment offers another opportunity to be present and mindful.

Likewise, if you can reside fully in the moment, you'll be freed from the tyranny of all past moments and all ideas about future ones.

108. "You Only Have Moments to Live"

Do you live as though you have all the time in the world? Having all the time in the world is, of course, an illusion. You never know what might happen— an accident, an illness, or a disaster. If you only had moments to live, would you change your priorities? What would you do? Where would you go? How would you interact with your family, friends, loved ones—even strangers? But truly: Why are you not doing these things now?

Often our preoccupation with the past or the future prevents our living the present. And in an important way, each moment is our "last" moment. Jon Kabat-Zinn explains in his magnum opus, *Coming to Our Senses*, these last moments are also, in a literal sense, the only place you *can* live. Life is lived now, no matter where the mind is.

Mindfulness practice trains you to be aware of these moments. It helps you to become intimate with these moments. Mindfulness can help you to make contact with these moments and claim them. It can move you from an abstract appreciation of life to a direct experience of it. Mindfulness practice trains the mind to be curious, even fascinated, with the ordinary moments of life—the simple feeling of breathing and bodily sensations, the taste of coffee, a rainy day, and so on. Mindfulness practice trains the mind to sit still and to come back to now—to this ordinary moment. It trains the mind to rest in the moment without having to chase after stimulation, acquisition, and stories of a life that is not happening now.

So: why not fully live this moment, right now, as if it were your very last? And this one. And this one.

On and on, one moment following the next, just so.

Afterword

I hope that mindfulness and mindfulness meditation practice will be an ongoing part of your life, and that these metaphors will help you to remember and to stay with practice.

May you get your doggy mind to behave and know the fiery spirit of Fierce Attention.

May you taste the tranquility of a still forest pool and be the leader of your pack.

May you avoid the man trap and get rid of your emotional baggage.

May you enjoy your seat and sharpen your axe.

May you befriend your petty tyrants and benefit from your wild chickens.

Acknowledgments

This book is dedicated to all of my patients and students, past and present. These metaphors emerged out of doing the work that I love, and you have all played a part in bringing this collection together. Special thanks go to James Julian, PhD, my graduate school advisor, who turned me on to the slim volume that has had the most impact on my graduate school career and beyond—*Metaphors We Live By*, which laid the foundation for this book. A heartfelt thanks goes to Elinore Standard, whose firm and encouraging editing made this book clearer and concise. Thanks also to my friends Polly Young-Eisendrath, Trina Hikel, and Sondra Solomon for their reading, comments, and encouragement. More thanks go to my students Emily McLaughlin, Stephanie Pollack, and Brittany Porter for their careful reading of the manuscript and editorial contributions. Reverend Taihaku Gretchen Priest and

Shinzen Young, two teachers from whom I have had the fortune to learn, deserve special thanks for reading an early draft. Particular thanks go to Larry Rosenberg for his years of inspirational teaching and guidance.

My Wisdom editor, Josh Bartok, merits a special thanks for recognizing the value of this book and for his comprehensive and patient editing.

Appendices:

Instructions and Exercises
for Mindfulness Meditation

Appendix 1: Mindful Breathing

To begin mindfulness practice, get into a comfortable seated posture. You can sit cross-legged on a cushion on the floor, if that is comfortable, or in a chair. You can practice mindfulness standing up, lying down, and walking (see instructions for Mindful Walking in appendix 3). A supportive posture with a straight back will allow breathing to happen unencumbered. Try to strike a posture and attitude that is open, dignified, and curious.

You can close your eyes or you can keep them slightly open, focusing softly on a spot a few feet in front of the body. Select a time to practice when you will be less likely to fall asleep and less likely to be disturbed by others. You may want to turn the ringers off on phones and turn off your cell phone if you can.

The process of getting ready to practice is called *taking your seat*, and it consists of both the physical posture and the *intention* to check in on your experience. Start by bringing attention to the way your breathing feels now, and notice its physical sensations. Try to be as descriptive of these sensations as you can. That is, note the physical properties instead of your opinions or preferences. Like the mapmaker, try not to be for or against any features you find. Rather, notice each feature of the landscape as accurately as possible.

You can concentrate attention on one point such as the upper lip, or the air moving through the nose. Alternatively, you can attend to the breath in a broad way—the overall process of breathing—remaining focused on its physical proprieties at all times. Whether you choose a narrow or a broad focus, work with the natural breath, the breath as it moves in the moment without trying to make it a relaxing breath or a special breath in any way. Taking your seat includes giving yourself permission to devote your attention in this way. The practice is to keep returning to the feelings of breathing whenever attention wanders.

The mind will surely wander and this is to be expected, and in no way suggests you are doing the practice improperly or that something is wrong with your mind. The mind may not want to sit still in this way and you may find that you are fetching and retrieving the mind, bringing it back to the seat repeatedly. The practice of bringing the mind back repeatedly is the key to mindfulness training.

As attention wanders away from the breath, as it inevitably will, see this, and with gentleness and kindness, usher attention back to the breath. There's no defeat in having the mind wander; it is a natural feature of the mind and it happens to all minds. So, pay attention to this process of moving away from the breath and coming back to the breath. As you do so, you will become familiar with this movement of attention, coming back again and again, and cultivating a sense of patience and gentleness with yourself.

Using the breath as an object of meditation has certain advantages. First, the breath is always with you and always available to you as an object of attention. You can't forget to bring it with you; you don't need any special props or conditions to meditate. The breath is your constant companion, ally, and friend. If you're not breathing, then you have bigger problems to deal with than practicing meditation!

Second, breathing is a good choice because awareness of breathing brings you into the body, and the body lives in the present moment. By focusing on breathing, you come into the body and the wisdom of the present. Coming into the body allows you to shift your awareness from future and past-oriented stories and negative critical commentaries of the present into the actual happening of the moment. The body is always experiencing some feeling, there are always sensations occurring in the body, and these comprise the experience of now.

Third, your breathing is often a reflection of the emotional state you are in. Breathing is affected by anxiety and stress. Noticing the feelings of breathing on a regular basis provides an early warning system when you move into states of anxiety or stress.

While focusing on breathing, other sensations in the body may arise and ask for attention. These may be uncomfortable feelings or pain. If that happens, and you are able to bring attention back to the breath, do that. If, however, that sensation is particularly intense, let the awareness of the breath move into the background, and allow attention to rest on the intense sensation for a moment. You can even try to give the breath to that sensation and imagine the breath flowing in and through that sensation. Sounds will also arise and compete for your attention. See if you can let the sounds be there along with the breath sensations without having to pay attention to them. Again, don't resist or struggle with what is happening. Try to return to the friendly embrace of the breath.

When you find that the sitting position has become uncomfortable, see if you can hold that discomfort and come back to the breath. However, it's best not to get consumed by a struggle, and there is no inherent virtue of remaining perfectly still. If you need to move the posture, do it with intention, awareness, and gentleness. In other words, when you move, move with mindfulness. The essence of this practice is to not fight with your experience and to not resist what is present. Try to open fully to your experience in every moment.

Another distraction that might arise is feelings of impatience, restlessness, or boredom. Typically, this happens when the mind projects itself into the future or tries to make this practice into something other than this simple looking at the breath. You can acknowledge these feelings, without buying into their stories. In response to impatience, restlessness, and boredom, you can give yourself permission to be with the breath, and return to the present without needing to make this moment anything more than it actually is.

Come back to this moment as it unfolds. You are learning about your mind and how it works, the sensations, thoughts, feelings, and images that emerge, and how there is a tendency to move away from the present moment. In response, try to give yourself permission not to get frustrated or discouraged. Keep coming back to the feelings of the breath. That's the practice.

Remember that awareness of breathing can happen at any time, not just when you sit down to meditate. Throughout the day, many times a day, you can try to remember yourself in this way. You can touch the breath, bringing awareness to a few cycles of the breath as you are hurrying through the day or coping with something stressful. You can bring yourself into the now by giving your attention to the breath. Come back to the formal practice described above as a way to strengthen your awareness and your ability to remember to be mindful throughout the rest of your experience (see appendix 5 on Informal Practice).

Appendix 2: Body-Scan Meditation

Mindfulness of bodily sensations or the Body-Scan Meditation continues the basic practice of Breathing Meditation and extends it to the entire body. The Body-Scan can be done systematically as a "guided tour" of the body. It can also be done with the body as a whole, by paying attention to sensations wherever in the body they arise. Or, you can sweep the body from the tips of the toes to the top of the head and back again.

The Body-Scan is a practice of paying exquisite attention to sensations occurring throughout the body, including the sensations of breathing. It is a way of exploring the complete experience of the body as you find it at the time of practice. Similar to mindfulness of breathing, it is a way to explore your experience with curiosity. It provides you with an opportunity to be fully with your experience as it unfolds moment by moment.

The Body-Scan is also an opportunity to practice mindfulness, "taking your seat" in the lying down or sitting orientation. Try practicing each way. If lying down, find a surface that is comfortable and support-ive, that is neither too hard nor too soft. Let your arms lie at the sides of the body and let your feet fall away from the body. Give the body over to the surface and let the surface reach up to support the body. If sitting, sit in a straight back chair or on a cushion on the floor and observe the body in this way. The posture should be comfortable and supportive for the practice. As with mindfulness of breathing, the posture is secondary to the intention you bring to practice. Select a time to practice when you will be less likely to fall asleep and less likely to be disturbed by others. If you can, turn off ringers and turn off your cell phone.

When you move attention through the rest of the body, try to follow these guidelines. You may notice both obvious and subtle sensations. In some areas, you may not notice much at all. Don't make this into a problem. The body will feel differently each time you check in and really look at it. Endeavor to greet whatever you find or don't find with the same open welcoming attention. Try to be a good host for your experience whatever that experience is in the moment.

What sorts of sensations are present in each region of the body? You may notice tingling or warm sensations, dull or sharp sensations, or nothing much at all. The sensations may be noticeable at the surface or within the body. Again, remember to greet whatever you find there with acceptance and curiosity. This is the general approach. As you move through the body, you will examine it in this sort of exacting detail. It's not the idea of the body but the actual sensations you are aiming for with your attention.

As you move through the body, try to give your attention to the part of the body that is the focus of the moment. However, from time to time other sensations in the body may compete for that attention. Something you identify as pain might arise and demand attention. If this occurs, you can let that sensation be present and bring attention back to the area of focus. If it is too intense and too distracting, you can move attention there and give it your full attention. Explore it and describe it at a physical level, noticing what is present and what it feels like. The goal is to be descriptive (for example, "sharp," "dull," "throbbing," "tight") rather than judgmental (for example, "I can't believe how much that hurts," "it's ruining my day"). After exploring the pain for a while, you can try to bring attention back to the area that is the focus of the moment in the sequence of the Body-Scan.

Whenever the mind wanders and attention has gone into storytelling, commentary, thinking, or worrying, bring it back to the sensations of what is happening in the body right now. If at any time sensations anywhere in the body become too intense or too difficult to approach, you can always bring attention to the breath. The breath moving in the background is a steady companion—a refuge that you can always touch, to anchor and reconnect you.

You can follow the following sequence through the body or you can develop your own sequence: Begin practice by drawing your attention to the interior of your experience, starting with the process of breathing. This is the physical aspect of breathing—the sensations caused by the breath moving on the lips and in the nose, throat, chest, and the belly. Give your attention to breathing without trying to make it any particular way; without trying to make it a relaxed breath, or your idea of what breathing should be like during meditation. Just let it be as it is, giving it your full attention. Try to be curious about the breath; what does it feel like? What does it actually feel like? Give your full attention to the process of breathing, letting awareness sink into the breath, loosening your grip on thinking, planning, anticipating, moving into the future, and holding on to the past.

When the mind wanders, which it will, into thinking planning, commenting, and chattering, bring it back to the here and now feelings of the breath, its physical qualities, and the raw sensations of the breath. Remember to be kind and understand that your mind, as all minds, will wander. That's what they do. Let me repeat that: *All minds wander.*

The goal of this practice is not to maintain perfect unbroken concentration, but rather to notice the extracurricular activities of the mind and the moving in and moving out of attention. Whenever it wanders, gently bring it back. Seeing it go and bringing it back repeatedly is the goal of practice. In addition, try to do this without impatience or frustration. The challenge is to be gentle with yourself. From the breath, direct your attention to the toes of the left foot and notice what's happening there. From the foot, move into the ankle with the same curiosity. From the ankle, explore the lower leg (the calf and the shin), and then the knee, and so on. The sequence goes from the knee into the upper leg, and then goes back over the leg as a whole, sweeping attention from the top of the leg to the tip of the toes and back again. From the left leg, you'll then move to the right leg and begin again with the toes. Repeat as you did for the left leg. Once the left leg is complete, you'll move to the pelvic region, including the buttocks, the genitals, and the hips.

From the pelvic region, you can move into the upper torso, investigating the low back and the abdominal area. Once you move back into the abdominal area, you'll once again notice the process of breathing. You might notice your belly expanding with air as the diaphragm engages. Then move into the area of the sternum and the mid back, and once again you'll feel the breath moving in this part of the body. Allow the breath to be natural, and feel those sensations in the center of the body to the middle of the back.

Next explore the upper back, the shoulder blades, and the chest—the entire upper torso. Find the breath moving in the area of the chest. Feel the entire torso at once; low back, mid back, and upper back, the belly, and the chest.

There may be uncomfortable sensations in the body, and you now have an opportunity to look at these and to see what sensations they are composed of. When you investigate these uncomfortable sensations, do so with curiosity, as a scientist would study some phenomenon. If there is an intense sensation, you can notice its intensity rather than becoming caught up in the storyline of that sensation or the label you give to that sensation. Instead, you can be with the experience of it.

From the torso move to both hands, paying attention to the fingers of the left and right hand, notice the sensations in each of the fingers, then the palms, and the tops of the hands. From there, move to the wrists, the forearms, the upper arms, the shoulders, and into the muscles surrounding the neck. Then feel the arms at once, from the tips of the fingers to the shoulders. Move to the neck, starting with the front of the neck, the back of the neck. Once again feel the presence of the breath in the interior of the body. Then feel the entire throat; note whatever sensations are present and whatever sense of energy is present.

Remember to keep your attention fluid and curious. Let awareness of the arms, shoulders, and neck rest in the background and move attention from the throat to the jaw and the teeth. Investigate the mouth, the tongue, the lips, the cheeks, the nose, around the eyes, and the ears. From the ears, move to the forehead, the scalp, and the entire head. Feel the breath again, moving through the nasal passages and mouth, and the entire head.

From the head, move through the entire body in a fluid sweeping motion. Sweep from the head into the neck and shoulders, arms, torso with the chest and the belly, back, pelvis, the legs, through the knees into the feet, and from the toes back through the feet and back through the legs and the knees, hips, torso, shoulders, arms, neck, throat, and head. Keep attention fluid and moving and note whatever is noticed as you move back and forth, top to bottom, bottom to top.

While doing this practice on your own, you will have to experiment with timing. Traditionally, Body-Scan meditation takes approximately forty minutes, but you can let it take longer or shorter, depending on your inclination and how much time you have for it. Even a very brief Body-Scan can be helpful.

Each time you complete the Body-Scan you have investigated your experience of the body as it exists now. By doing this practice, you'll develop clarity and curiosity toward your body. I hope that this meditation will be a part of your daily routine.

Appendix 3: Walking Meditation

Walking Meditation is another basic form of mindfulness practice. Being mindful while walking gives you the opportunity to practice mindfulness as you move and can also give you additional opportunities to practice as you go through your day. Walking meditation can be done as a practice in itself, or in alternating fashion with the seated Breathing Meditation. For example, do sitting practice for thirty to forty-five minutes and then do mindful walking for fifteen minutes in recurring cycles.

Mindful Walking practice can be done a couple of ways. One way is to walk at a normal pace and to pay attention to the sensations in the body that occur while walking. Similar to Mindful Breathing, bring attention back to these sensations or the sensations of the breath whenever the mind wanders. The alternative is to do slow forms of walking. In these slow motion practices, you coordinate the steps of walking with the process of breathing.

In one variation of this practice, take one step on the in-breath and another step on the out-breath. Continue to walk in that way, coordinating steps with breath, stepping with one foot as you breathe in, and stepping with the other foot as you breathe out. Make sure that steps are coordinated to the breath and not the other way around. The process of coordinating steps with breath can be slowed down even further. On the in-breath, lift one foot up; on the out-breath place the foot back down. To slow the process even further still, on the in-breath, lift the heel off the floor; on the out-breath, lift the toes and move the foot, and on the next in breath place the foot down. Experiment with the different forms and paces. When you are in an agitated frame of mind, it can be helpful to try slow walking. If you are sleepy or tired, it can be helpful to walk at a more vigorous pace.

As with Mindful Breathing and the Body-Scan, the key to practice is to stay with the sensations in the body and with the experience of walking and of moving, instead of thinking about it or telling stories. Remember, it is not the *idea* of walking but the *actual experience* of it.

Slow walking can be done by walking back and forth in a "track" laid out on the floor, or in a circle. It can also be done outside but, be forewarned, very slow walking will attract attention! To walk in a track, set out a span on the floor, perhaps ten or twelve feet, in a straight line. Do the walking along the track and at the end, stop, and take a mindful breath. Turn around mindfully and continue walking back along the track. Walking in a circular pattern provides a continuous movement. The distance can be adjusted as needed. But remember, you are not trying to *get anywhere*, so more steps or more ground covered is not the goal.

Whichever pace and style you choose, maintain a continuity of awareness and contact with the breath, and when attention wanders, kindly usher it back to the experience of walking and breathing.

Come back into the body whenever attention wanders. Be with the walking as it unfolds step by step. This walking practice is mindfulness in action and provides you with a portable way to practice. It can be done just about anywhere or anytime. It can be a particularly helpful practice, if you are somewhere

where you have to wait, provided you are able to move around. You can also enjoy moments of mindfulness as you walk to and from places throughout your day, even as you move from room to room at the office or at home, or the span from your car to your destination.

You are not trying to get anywhere or to achieve anything. You are simply being and simply walking.

Appendix 4: Relationship Practice

If you are in a relationship, you can try the following exercises with your partner—you can also do it with a friend or a family member.

Facing one another, sit in silence together, trying to be mindful, coming back from the storytelling mind each time thoughts start to coalesce. You can start with eyes closed and then move to eyes open. Keep attention on looking, feeling, and listening.

Then take turns describing everything you are aware of in the moment. For instance, you could describe how the chair feels on your buttocks, how you feel self-conscious doing this exercise, how you feel warm, and so forth. The partner remains silent, looking, feeling, and listening.

Then switch.

Next, describe a relatively neutral event that occurred earlier in the day, perhaps what you had for breakfast or a mundane incident from work. While you are describing this event, try to stay with the sensations in the moment as you did in the previous part. This will be challenging and you'll find the mind getting lost quite often. With patience, come back and keep trying. You'll also find that you need to slow things down a bit to stay connected mindfully with feelings during an interactive exercise like this.

Take turns describing this neutral event. For the next round, move to describing some event that has some emotional heat to it, perhaps some difficult feeling for a third party, such as your boss or your child. Proceed with the description trying to stay in contact with feelings in the body. The breath is a good target. With practice, it can feel as though you are talking through the breath.

This practice has two major benefits. The first is that it helps you to be less reactive. It builds in opportunities for pausing. The second and related benefit is that by helping you to be less reactive, social interactions and difficult situations will feel less stressful. Talking through the breath serves as a buffer. The next round of exercises can focus on difficult issues with your partner. After much practice, and when you can maintain some degree of mindful awareness through the earlier interactions, you can move on to this more difficult exercise. Being mindful in this way helps to create healthy boundaries between people.

These boundaries are based on respect and recognition of each other's autonomy.

When you can be mindful, you are telling your partner that you will be his or her guardian of solitude in that moment because you are coming to him or her without a hidden agenda, attuned to what is happening in the present.

Appendix 5: Informal Practice

Finding time to practice is one of the key challenges for integrating mindfulness into daily life. Formal practice "on the cushion" whether sitting, walking, lying down, or standing is crucial for establishing a foundation of mindfulness that can be harvested in your life off of the cushion. Fortunately, in addition to whatever time you can carve out of your busy life to do formal practice, there are abundant opportunities to engage in practice informally. In fact, most moments of your life can be recruited as opportunities for practicing and cultivating mindfulness.

Think about what you do during a typical day. You awake, you shower, you get dressed, you eat, you commute, you walk, you prepare meals, you eat meals, and you wash dishes. Each of these activities can be practice. Any activity can be one of mindfulness if you work in a deliberate way with your storytelling mind. You simply aim to give your full attention to whatever activity is occurring in the moment. The storytelling mind will probably not comply with this effort and will start to engage in all sorts of past- and future-oriented musings. Pay attention to the shift from the here-and-now of the activity to the there-and-then thoughts of the storytelling mind. With gentleness and kindness, bring attention back to what is happening now. Monitor yourself in this way.

It comes down to a choice that you can make in any given moment to be awake to your experience. Most of what the storytelling mind engages with isn't all that compelling. When anxious, the incessant chattering of the storytelling mind runs tapes of regret and worry. You certainly can do with less of this.

Try to incorporate these opportunities for being awake and practicing throughout the day. When waking, be mindful of the sensations of the body; when showering be mindful of the experience of showering, the feelings of water and the sounds; when dressing be mindful of dressing; when eating be mindful of eating; when driving be mindful of the experience of driving, giving your full attention to this experience, paying exquisite attention to the sights and sounds of the road, and the feelings in the body that accompany driving; when walking one place to another, be mindful of walking, of the things you see, hear, and smell while walking and of the feelings in the body, including the breath.

When at work, you have ample opportunities to be mindful. Use your appointment technology to schedule appointments with mindfulness. Try to take a fraction of each hour, perhaps five minutes, to sit and be with the breath and the sensations in the body. Try to give full attention to whatever task is at hand, whether this is sitting in a meeting or talking to a client. Certainly, there may be opportunities to be mindful while walking from one place to another, while sitting at your desk, or while doing whatever activities are involved in your work.

As you go through these various activities you can pay attention to the experience itself, to the overall feeling of working, walking, or washing dishes. You can also pay attention to the sensations in the body and breath that accompany the experience. Attention can move seamlessly between these places to focus. The key is to stay out of the storytelling mind.

Practice mindfulness on the spot whenever moments of tension arise in the course of the day. Steal a few breaths away from the storytelling mind to create a noticeable shift in your well-being. You can also bring mindful attention to particular activities that are suited to bringing you to mindfulness, such as listening to music, reading poetry, looking at art, and eating.

Eating is a special opportunity to practice mindfulness. See if you can give your full attention to what you eat. Pay close attention to the way the food looks, feels, smells, and sounds in addition to the actual taste of the food. You may want to experiment with eating slowly so you can enjoy the sensory qualities of the food. When attention wanders into thinking about the food or something else, bring it back to the sensory qualities of the food.

Enjoy!

Notes

Introduction

"This incisive work shaped..." The use of metaphor in psychotherapy is explored in Kozak 1992. This paper was one of my master's theses and was also the Student Award Winner, APA Division 24: Theoretical and Philosophical Psychology (National competition for outstanding student paper, award presented at the 1992 APA convention).

"We understand the world..." Jaynes 1976, 52, discussed the felt experience of meaning: "Understanding a thing is to arrive at a metaphor for that thing by substituting something more familiar to us. And the feeling of familiarity is the feeling of understanding."

"In this way, concepts are not arbitrary..." as developed in Gallese and Lakoff 2005, and Lakoff and Johnson 1999.

"Metaphor is the very ground of language..." Likewise, the philosopher Friedrich Nietzsche recognized that the basic mental activity of categorization relied upon metaphors. For example, the mind has a "metaphoric" concept for leaf that recognizes all leaves, even though no two leaves are exactly the same. Nietzsche also felt that metaphor had profound implications for how the world is perceived and experienced, and that much of what passes for literal language is old, worn out metaphors.

"*To be* has the same etymological..." Jaynes 1976, 51, goes on to say "It is something of a lovely surprise that the irregular conjugation of our most nondescript verb is a record of a time when man had no independent word for 'existence' and could only say that something 'grows' or that it 'breathes.'"

Reading This Book

"Each of the 108..." 108 is a number that has attracted the attention of mathematicians for its unique properties. For example, the interior angles for an equilateral pentagon measure 108 degrees each. It is also regarded as sacred in Hinduism and Buddhism, among other religions. Hindu deities such as Shiva are known to have 108 names, and there are 108 beads in a prayer *mala* (akin to a rosary). It also represents the number of Buddhist realized saints (*arhats*) or sins or defilements of the mind in Tibetan Buddhism. The origins of 108 is speculative but it may represent its intrinsic mathematical properties such as it is the product of 1^1 by 2^2 by 3^3 or perhaps as a reflection of the relative distance of the earth to the moon (approximately 108) and the relative distance of the earth to the sun is 108 times the sun's diameter (and also the number of times greater the sun's diameter is of the earth's). Since mindfulness emerges from the Buddhist traditions, I thought 108 would be a fitting number.

Metaphors for Mind

"It is virtually impossible..." Lakoff and Johnson 1999, 235.

"From this perspective..." Lakoff and Johnson 1999, 5, reveal that "Real human beings are not, for the most part, in conscious control of—or even consciously aware of—their reasoning. Most of their reason, besides, is based on various kinds of prototypes, framings, and metaphors. People seldom engage in a form of economic reason that could maximize utility."

2. The Four-Floor Building

"Categorization is a convenient…" Lakoff and Johnson 1999, 20, argue that categorization is constrained by the hardware of human neural systems. For instance, the eye reduces information by a factor of 100 to 1. You can't possibly deal with all the information that is available in any given moment. At best, only a fraction can be noticed in any given moment.

"Almost one hundred years ago…" James 1911, 51.

4. Doggy Mind and Monkey Mind

"Doggy Mind runs after bone…" comes from a dharma talk given by Larry Rosenberg at the Insight Meditation Society in August of 1992. The full *gata* goes:

> Doggy Mind runs after bone
> Lion Mind unimpressed
> Spider Mind weaves endless web

"This is doggy mind…" is also discussed in Rosenberg 1998, 22.

6. Friendly Neighborhood Spider Mind

"This is the enlightenment of the ordinary mind." See, for example, Magid 2002.

7. Carving Nature at the Joints
"In many ways such learning..." Siegel 2007, 105–6.

9. The Inner Mute Button
"These can arise individually..." These designations come from Young 2007.

12. Waking Up
"Some have called this state..." The psychologist and consciousness researcher, Charles Tart (1994, 73), put it this way:

> There is a social contract we implicitly live under. Most of us are asleep, are relatively mindless, are living in our waking dreams because that was the best we could do to protect against suffering, against the mindless assault on our essence when we were children. Someone who begins to show some signs of awakening can be very disturbing to people who are still heavily defended and deeply asleep.

18. Form and Emptiness
"It could just as easily be translated..." Glassman 2003.

Metaphors for Self

"As with the mind..." "Have you taken a good look at yourself recently? Do you have a hidden self that you are trying to protect or that is so awful you don't want anyone to know about it? If you have ever considered any matters of this sort, you have been relying on unconscious models of what a self is, and you could hardly live a life of any introspection at all without doing so" (Lakoff and Johnson 1999, 10).

"It is helpful to make a distinction..." According to Lakoff and Johnson (1999, 268):

> The Subject is the locus of consciousness, subjective experience, reason, will, and our "essence," everything that makes us who we uniquely are. There is at least one Self and possibly more. The Selves consist of everything else about us—our bodies, our social roles, our histories, and so on.

"The subject is always..." Lakoff and Johnson, 1999, emphasis original.

20. A Flashlight in a Dark Room
"Consciousness is a much smaller..." Jaynes 1976, 23.

21. Witness
"As Shunryu Suzuki says..." Suzuki 1970, 134.

23. Thoughts Like Soap Bubbles
"What emerges is closer..." Kabat-Zinn 2005, 321–9.

32. Quorum
"The Tibetan Buddhist teacher..." Sogyal Rinpoche 1995, April 19 entry.

"Harvard neuroscientist Stephen Pinker..." Pinker 1997, 58.

Metaphors for Emotion, Change, and "Ordinary Craziness"

"It can also helpful for..." The research on mindfulness-based interventions for diagnosable psychiatric conditions includes effectiveness for anxiety disorders, preventing the recurrence of major depression, obsessive compulsive disorder, eating disorders, substance abuse, borderline personality disorder, etc.

34. The Uncertain Fire
"The idea of choosing..." I have always thought the Ben & Jerry's bumper sticker: "If it's not fun why do it?" needed a caveat on maintaining responsibilities.

"In order not to leave..." Suzuki 1970, 63.

37. Guardianship of Solitude
"It is a question in marriage..." Rilke 1975, 28, emphasis original.

40. Deprivation Mind

"The meditation teacher…" Ram Dass, aka Richard Alpert, Ph.D., was a professor of psychology at Harvard University in the early 1960s. He and his colleague, Timothy Leary, were fired for liberal experimentation with LSD. Later, Ram Dass traveled to India to study yoga and returned to the United States to become an author and teacher. His best-known book, *Be Here Now*, has sold over one million copies.

41. "I've Got Good News and I've Got Bad News"

"This is the notorious…" One researcher, Taylor 2006, has suggested an alternative to fight or flight— tend and befriend, which may be more characteristic of female members of a species.

"In fact, this 'legacy brain'…" The legacy brain refers to the finding that humans evolved in an environment that existed 100,000 years ago.

"Understanding what the stress…" For further reading on stress, I recommend Sapolsky's *Why Zebras Don't Get Ulcers*, which is a readable work by a leading stress researcher, and McEwan and Lasley's *The End of Stress as We Know It*, by another pair of stress researchers.

44. "Ninety Miles An Hour is the Speed I Drive"

From the lyrics of the Jimi Hendrix song "Crosstown Traffic" on the album *Electric Ladyland*, 1968.

50. Cleopatra Syndrome
"I'm not here, this isn't happening." From the Radiohead song "How to Disappear Completely" on *Kid A*, 2000.

51. "Please Pass the Tums"
"Marley: 'Why do you…'" Dickens 2007.

55. The Investing Dentist
"He feels a pang…" Taleb 2001, 57.

56. "Might As Well Face it, You're Addicted to Thoughts"
"The meditation teacher…" Chögyam Trungpa 1996, 54.

58. Babysitting
"A therapeutic intervention called…" see Segal, Williams, and Teasdale 2003.

59. "Move It or Lose It!"
"This process is called habituation…" So, why is it that you can look at something for a long time and it doesn't disappear? According to Passer and Smith 2004, 114, a fascinating characteristic of vision explains this—the image on the retina moves constantly. By doing so, habituation is prevented. You are not aware of this movement, but psychologists have devised clever experiments that can stabilize the movement of the image hitting the retina and voila,

the image disappears! In order to create a stabilized retinal image, an experimental subject would wear a special contact lens that has a tiny projector attached. Despite normal eye movements, images are cast on the same region of the retina. When this experiment is conducted, the image is clear at first but then begins to fade and reappear as receptors in the retina fatigue and recover.

Metaphors for Acceptance, Resistance, and Space

66. Weeds
"You should be rather…" Suzuki 1970, 36.

70. "Revolting! Give me some more."
"In the beginner's mind…" Suzuki 1970, 21.

"We get to observe his…" As is typical for both media and academic writing, the terms for emotion and feeling are used interchangeably. Brown and Kozak (1998) argue there are important functional distinctions between feeling and emotion. What Data is reporting in the vignette would be considered feeling, not emotions.

71. To Give Your Sheep Or Cow A Large Meadow
     Is The Way To Control Him
"To give your sheep…" Suzuki 1970, 31.

73. The Sole of the Earth
"A wise counsel to her suggested..." Khyentse 2007.

75. Petty Tyrants
"There is a story about..." This story of the tea-servant was presented in Kornfield 1998.

You probably don't have to go out of your way to find petty tyrants; life has a tendency to provide them in abundance. But this should not be taken as encouragement to stay in an abusive or dysfunctional relationship, for instance. Rather, it reflects the counterintuitive wisdom that no matter the circumstance, there is always something we can work with. Sometimes the relationship is unavoidable, such as when the Chinese invaded Tibet in 1949. At that time, Mao Tse Tung became His Holiness the Dalai Lama's petty tyrant.

80. "Bring Me a Mustard Seed"
"The Buddha was known..." In fact, the Buddha did not see himself as the founder of a religion, and he did not view the practices he taught as religion. They could be more accurately described as a process of scientific self-inquiry. He discouraged his students from taking anything on faith and required that all students test things out for themselves.

"One day, a young woman..." The story of Kisa Gotami is presented in Goss and Klass 1997.

82. "Why Didn't I Kneel More Deeply to Accept You?"

"Why didn't I kneel..." These lines come from the "Tenth Duino Elegy," Rilke 1989, 205, translated by Stephen Mitchell.

86. Mental Aikido

"The aims of Aikido moves..." were presented in an article by Stevens 2007, 70.

Metaphors for Practice

92. The Stillness Between Two Waves of the Sea

"In certain meditation traditions..." Trungpa 1996.

94. Sharpening the Axe

"Mindfulness meditation practice..." The axe metaphor comes from Young 2005.

97. Learning To Play A Musical Instrument

"It is said that it takes..." The finding of 10,000 hours comes from the research of Ericcson et al. 1993.

"As few as eight weeks..." Davidson et al. 2003.

98. "Just Do It!"

A complete set of free guided meditations is available at exquisitemind.com/practice.html

108. "You Only Have Moments to Live"

"Mindfulness practice trains you…" This is not to say that you should not have goals, ambitions, and aspirations. Planning can be an activity done in the present. Instead, I am referring to the unproductive tendency to wish things could have been different.

Appendices

Appendix 4: Relationship Practice

"Keep attention on…" The exercise of sensing (or feeling), looking, and listening comes from Charles Tart 1994, 56. If you think about it, in any given moment you are doing one or the other or all three of these things. There will be things you see (provided your eyes are open), things you hear, and there will be feelings in the body.

Works Cited

Armstrong, Karen. 2001. *Buddha*. New York: Penguin.

Brown, Terrance A., and Arnold Kozak. 1998. Emotion and the possibility of psychologists entering into heaven. In *What develops in emotional development?*, ed. Michael F. Mascolo and Sharon Griffin, 135–55. New York: Plenum Press.

Castaneda, Carlos. 1991. *Fire from within*. New York: Pocket.

Chödrön, Pema. 2002. *The places that scare you*. Boston: Shambhala.

Davidson, Richard J., Jon Kabat-Zinn, Jessica Schumacher, Melissa Rosenkranz, Daniel Muller, Saki F. Santorelli, Ferris Urbanowski, Anne Harrington, Katherine Bonus, and John F. Sheridan. 2003. Alterations in brain and immune function produced by mindfulness meditation. *Psychosomatic Medicine* 65: 564–70.

Dawkins, Richard. 2006. *The god delusion*. New York: Houghton Mifflin.

Dickens, Charles. *A Christmas Carol*. Retrieved June 27, 2007, from http://www.literature.org/authors/dickens-charles/christmas-carol/chapter-01.html

Eliot, T.S. 1943. *Four quartets*. New York: Harvest.

Epstein, Mark. 2001 (March/April). All You Can Eat. *Yoga Journal*. Retrieved June 27, 2007, from http://www.yogajournal.com/lifestyle/11

Ericcson, K. Anders, Ralf Th. Krampe, and Clemens Tesch-Romer. 1993. The role of deliberate practice in the acquisition of expert performance. *Psychology Review* 100 (3): 366–406.

Fronsdal, Gil. 2005. *The Dhammapada*. Boston: Shambhala.

Fischer-Schreiber, Ingrid, Franz-Karl Ehrhard, and Michael S. Diener. 1991. *The Shambhala dictionary of Buddhism and Zen*. Boston: Shambhala.

Germer, Christopher K., Ronald D. Siegel, and Paul R. Fulton, eds. 2005. *Mindfulness and psychotherapy*. New York: Guilford.

Gallese, Vittorio, and George Lakoff. 2005. The brain's concepts: the role of the sensory-motor system in conceptual knowledge. *Cognitive Neuropsychology* 22 (3/4): 455–79.

Glassman, Bernie. 2003. *Infinite circle: Teachings in Zen*. Boston: Shambhala.

Goss, Robert E., and Dennis Klass. 1997. Tibetan Buddhism and the resolution of grief: The *Bhardo Thodol* for the dying and grieving. *Death Studies* 21: 377–95.

James, William. 1911. *Some problems in philosophy*. New York: Longmans Green.

Jaynes, Julian. 1976. *The origins of consciousness in the breakdown of the bicameral mind*. New York: Houghton Mifflin.

Kabat-Zinn, Jon. 2005. *Coming to our senses*. New York: Hyperion.

Khyentse, Dongzer Jamyang. 2007 (January). "What makes you a Buddhist?" *Shambhala Sun*.

Kornfield, Jack. 1985. *A still forest pool: the insight meditation of Achaan Chah*. New York: Quest.

———. 1998. *The inner art of meditation*. Boulder, CO: Sounds True.

Kozak, Arnold. 1992. The epistemic consequences of embodied metaphor. *Theoretical and Philosophical Psychology* 12: 302–19.

Lakoff, George, and Mark Johnson. 1980. *Metaphors we live by*. Chicago: University of Chicago Press.

———. 1999. *Philosophy in the flesh*. New York: Basic Books.

Magid, Barry. 2002. *Ordinary mind: Exploring the common ground of Zen and psychotherapy*. Boston: Wisdom.

McEwan, Bruce, and Elizabeth Norton Lasley. 2004. *The end of stress as we know it*. Washington, D.C.: Dana Press.

Millan, Cesar. 2006. *Cesar's way: The natural, everyday guide to understanding and correcting common dog problems*. New York: Harmony.

Mipham, Sakyong. 2004. *Turning the mind into an ally*. New York: Riverhead Trade.

———. 2006. *Ruling your world: Ancient strategies for modern life*. New York: Broadway.

Newberg, Andres, and Eugene D'Auili. 2001. *Why god won't go away: brain science & the biology of belief*. New York: Ballantine.

Nietzsche, Friedrich. 1954. On truth and lie in an extra moral sense. In *The portable Nietzsche*, Ed. and Trans. Walter Kaufmann, 42–47. New York: Penguin. (Original work written 1873.)

Passer, Michael W., and Ronald E. Smith. 2004. *Psychology: The science of mind and behavior*. Boston: McGraw Hill.

Pinker, Steven. 1997. *How the mind works*. New York: Norton.

Rilke, Rainer Maria. 1975. *On love and other difficulties*. Ed. John L. Mood. New York: Norton.

Rilke, Rainer Maria. 1989. *Selected poetry of Rainer Maria Rilke*. Ed. and Trans. Stephen Mitchell. New York: Vintage International.

Rosenberg, Larry. 1998. *Breath by breath: The liberating practice of insight meditation.* Boston: Shambhala.

Sapolsky, Robert M. 2004. *Why zebras don't get ulcers,* Third Edition. New York: Owl.

Siegel, Daniel J. 2007. *The mindful brain.* New York: Norton.

Segal, Zindal V., J. Mark G. Williams, and John D. Teasdale. 2003. *Mindfulness-based cognitive therapy for depression.* New York: Guilford.

Sogyal Rinpoche. 1995. *Glimpse after glimpse.* San Francisco: Harper: SanFrancisco.

Stevens, John. 2007 (March). The art of peace. *Shambhala Sun,* 68–70.

Suzuki, Shunryu. 1970. *Zen mind, beginner's mind.* Boston: Weatherhill.

Taleb, Nassim Nicholas. 2001. *Fooled by randomness: the hidden role of randomness in the markets and life.* New York: Norton.

Tart, Charles C. 1994. *Living the mindful life.* Boston: Shambhala.

Taylor, Shelly. 2006. *Health psychology*. Boston: McGraw Hill.

Thoreau, Henry David. Retrieved June 27, 2007, from http://www.bartleby.com/66/18/60418.html.

Trungpa, Chögyam. 1996. *Meditation in action*. Boston: Shambhala.

Walcott, Derek. 1986. *Derek Walcott collected poems 1948–1984*. New York: Farrar.

Whyte, David. 2002. *Clear mind wild heart*. Boulder, CO: Sounds True.

Young, Shinzen . 2005. *Break through pain: A step-by-step mindfulness meditation program for transforming chronic and acute pain*. Boulder, CO: Sounds True.

Young, Shinzen. 2007. *What is mindfulness?* Retrieved July 27, 2007, from http://www.shinzen.org/shinsub3/What%20is%20Mindfulness.pdf

About the Author

ARNIE KOZAK is a clinical assistant professor in the Department of Psychiatry at the University of Vermont College of Medicine and a licensed psychologist–doctorate in the state of Vermont. He is a workshop leader at the Barre Center for Buddhist Studies, Kripalu Center for Yoga and Health, and the Copper Beech Institute. He is the author of multiple books including *Mindfulness A to Z: 108 Insights for Awakening Now*. Arnie has been practicing yoga and meditation for over thirty years and is dedicated to translating the Buddha's teachings into readily accessible forms. When he's not working, you can find him trail running with his dogs in the foothills of the Green Mountains. Visit arniekozak.com for information on upcoming workshops. Visit the "Practice" section of Dr. Kozak's site for ten hours of free guided meditations to support your mindfulness practice.

Also Available from Wisdom Publications

MINDFULNESS A TO Z
108 Insights for Awakening Now
Dr. Arnie Kozak

"You don't 'read' *Mindfulness A to Z*. Rather you go on a series of intimate journeys with author Arnie Kozak and explore the facets of heart and awareness that can free your spirit."
— Tara Brach, PhD, author of *True Refuge*

LIVING MINDFULLY
At Home, at Work, and in the World
Deborah Schoeberlein David

"A wonderful introduction to a most beneficial approach to living a life. Reading the book is like being on retreat with a wise and practical teacher."
—Kathleen Dowling Singh, author of *The Grace in Aging*

MINDFULNESS IN PLAIN ENGLISH
Bhante Gunaratana

"A classic—one of the very best English sources for author-itative explanations of mindfulness."
—Daniel Goleman, author of *Emotional Intelligence*

KINDFULNESS
Ajahn Brahm

"In a stroke of genius, Ajahn Brahm turns mindfulness into kindfulness, a practice that opens our hearts to others as well as to ourselves."
—Toni Bernhard, author of *How to Be Sick*

About Wisdom Publications

Wisdom Publications is the leading publisher of classic and contemporary Buddhist books and practical works on mindfulness. To learn more about us or to explore our other books, please visit our website at wisdompubs.org or contact us at the address below.

Wisdom Publications
199 Elm Street
Somerville, MA 02144 USA

We are a 501(c)(3) organization, and donations in support of our mission are tax deductible.

Wisdom Publications is affiliated with the Foundation for the Preservation of the Mahayana Tradition (FPMT).